COMPUTERS AND
THE INTERNET

Computers and the Internet

EXAMINING POP CULTURE

JUDITH GALAS
Book Editor

Daniel Leone,
Publisher

Bonnie Szumski,
Editorial Director

Scott Barbour,
Managing Editor

James D. Torr,
Series Editor

Greenhaven Press, Inc.
San Diego, California

Library of Congress Cataloging-in-Publication Data

Computers and the internet / Judith C. Galas, book editor.
p. cm.—(Examining popular culture)
Includes bibliographical references and index.
ISBN 0-7377-0860-3 (pbk. : alk. paper).—
ISBN 0-7377-0861-1 (lib. bdg. : alk. paper).—
1. Computers and civilization. 2. Internet—Social aspects.
I. Galas, Judith C., 1946–   II. Series.

QA76.9.C66 C632   2002
306.48'34—dc21   2001023808
                                                            CIP

Cover Photo: © Tony Stone Images

© 2002 by Greenhaven Press, Inc.
PO Box 28909, San Diego, CA 92198–0990

Printed in the U.S.A.

CONTENTS

people too busy or too shy to obtain face-to-face dates.

Chapter 3: Transforming Popular Entertainment

such as credit card and medical reports, is stored
online, the right to privacy may be threatened.

Chapter 5: The Future of High Technology

FOREWORD

POPULAR CULTURE IS THE COMMON SET OF ARTS, entertainments, customs, beliefs, and values shared by large segments of society. Russel B. Nye, one of the founders of the study of popular culture, wrote that "not until the appearance of mass society in the eighteenth century could popular culture, as one now uses the term, be said to exist." According to Nye, the Industrial Revolution and the rise of democracy in the eighteenth and nineteenth centuries led to increased urbanization and the emergence of a powerful middle class. In nineteenth-century Europe and North America, these trends created audiences for the popular arts that were larger, more concentrated, and more well off than at any point in history. As a result, more people shared a common culture than ever before.

The technological advancements of the twentieth century vastly accelerated the spread of popular culture. With each new advance in mass communication—motion pictures, radio, television, and the Internet—popular culture has become an increasingly pervasive aspect of everyday life.

Popular entertainment—in the form of movies, television, theater, music recordings and concerts, books, magazines, sporting events, video games, restaurants, casinos, theme parks, and other attractions—is one very recognizable aspect of popular culture. In his 1999 book *The Entertainment Economy: How Mega-Media Forces Are Transforming Our Lives*, Michael J. Wolf argues that entertainment is becoming the dominant feature of American society: "In choosing where we buy French fries, how we relate to political candidates, what airline we want to fly, what pajamas we choose for our kids, and which mall we want to buy them in, entertainment is increasingly influencing every one of those choices. . . . Multiply that by the billions of choices that, collectively, all of us make each day and you have a portrait of a society in which entertainment is one of its leading institutions."

It is partly this pervasive quality of popular culture that makes it worthy of study. James Combs, the author of *Polpop: Politics and Popular Culture in America*, explains that examining popular culture is important because it can shape people's attitudes and beliefs:

> Popular culture is so much a part of our lives that we cannot deny its developmental powers. . . . Like formal education or family rearing, popular culture is part of our "learning environment.". . . Though our pop culture education is informal—we usually do not attend to pop culture for its "educational" value—it nevertheless provides us with information and images upon which we develop our opinions and attitudes. We would not be what we are, nor would our society be quite the same, without the impact of popular culture.

Examining popular culture is also important because popular movies, music, fads, and the like often reflect popular opinions and attitudes. Christopher D. Geist and Jack Nachbar explain in *The Popular Culture Reader*, "the popular arts provide a gauge by which we can learn what Americans are thinking, their fears, fantasies, dreams, and dominant mythologies. The popular arts reflect the values of the multitude."

This two-way relationship between popular culture and society is evident in many modern discussions of popular culture. Does the glorification of guns by many rap artists, for example, merely reflect the realities of inner-city life, or does it also contribute to the problem of gun violence? Such questions also arise in discussions of the popular culture of the past. Did the Vietnam protest music of the late 1960s and early 1970s, for instance, simply reflect popular antiwar sentiments, or did it help turn public opinion against the war? Examining such questions is an important part of understanding history.

Greenhaven Press's Examining Pop Culture series provides students with the resources to begin exploring these questions. Each volume in the series focuses on a particular aspect of popular culture, with topics as varied as popular culture itself. Books in the series may focus on a particular genre, such as *Rap and Hip Hop*, while others may cover a specific medium, such as *Computers and the Internet*. Volumes such as *Body Piercing and Tattoos* have their focus on recent trends in popular culture, while titles like *Americans' Views About War* have a broader historical scope.

In each volume, an introductory essay provides a general

overview of the topic. The selections that follow offer a survey of critical thought about the subject. The readings in *Americans' Views About War*, for example, are arranged chronologically: Essays explore how popular films, songs, television programs, and even comic books both reflected and shaped public opinion about American wars from World War I through Vietnam. The essays in *Violence in Film and TV*, on the other hand, take a more varied approach: Some provide historical background, while others examine specific genres of violent film, such as horror, and still others discuss the current controversy surrounding the issue.

Each book in the series contains a comprehensive index to help readers quickly locate material of interest. Perhaps most importantly, each volume has an annotated bibliography to aid interested students in conducting further research on the topic. In today's culture, what is "popular" changes rapidly from year to year and even month to month. Those who study popular culture must constantly struggle to keep up. The volumes in Greenhaven's Examining Pop Culture series are intended to introduce readers to the major themes and issues associated with each topic, so they can begin examining for themselves what impact popular culture has on their own lives.

INTRODUCTION

IN THEIR BOOK *THE DREAM MACHINE: EXPLORING the Computer Age*, authors John Palfreman and Doron Swade share a forecast from Howard Aiken, an American mathematician and computer engineer: In 1947, Aiken predicted that "only six electronic computers would be needed to satisfy all the United States' computing needs." Today, with more than 400 million personal computers in the world and a billion anticipated by 2005, Aiken's forecast seems laughable.

In 1944, Aiken and his colleagues from IBM and Harvard University created the Mark I, which many consider the first general-purpose computer. Fifty feet long and eight feet high, it cost $500,000, read data from punch cards, and spit out calculations at the then-astounding rate of about three to five a second.

Today, computers no larger than a slim-volumed book can process many thousands of bits of data per second and cost less than a thousand dollars. Compact, robust, and growing cheaper by the day, computers also do much more than calculate. They enable people to compose books and music, teach children their numbers and alphabet, trade stocks, communicate worldwide swiftly and cheaply, plan a trip and then virtually visit that vacation destination, and a myriad of other daily tasks.

Once used only by the military, computers have permeated almost every aspect of life. Microwaves, coffee pots, toys, autos, jet planes, satellites, and pacemakers—items small and large, trivial and essential—run on computers. It may be nearly impossible for those coming of age in the United States at the start of the twenty-first century to imagine life without computer technology. But millions of Americans remember a time—not so long ago—when computers did not even exist.

Life Before Computers

At the start of the twenty-first century, the average high school or college student likely has grandparents who were born in the 1930s. In that decade people saw the rise of two state-of-the-art communication tools. The first was the home radio. In 1930, about 60 percent of U.S. households owned one. Like the television of today, the home radio tuned families into the day's news and broadened their worldview. The second development was the ballpoint pen. By the end of the 1930s, people could write with ink without first dipping their pen's nib into an inkwell.

The parents of many of today's students likely were born in the 1960s, a time that saw many technological advancements in the fields of communication and computers. The first commercial copier came on the scene in 1959. The first industrial robots showed up at their factory jobs in 1962. The first cardiac pacemaker, which linked medicine to an integrated circuit, was developed in 1967.

In 1960, only about 6,000 computers were operating in the United States—not in homes or neighborhood schools and libraries, but in government offices and university research labs. In 1961, when President John F. Kennedy told Congress, "I believe we should go to the moon," he could announce his dream of space exploration because computers had begun to hum in government agencies. Computer software, as much as rocket science, would take man to the moon.

Just as the 1960s began with images of space travel, it ended with director Stanley Kubrick's film *2001: A Space Odyssey* and HAL, the computer that mutinied in space and took control of a spacecraft. In the more than three decades since HAL's monotone voice first chilled moviegoers, the dominance of computers in the world has seemed to move at warp speed.

The Personal Computer Emerges

In 1970, the first floppy disk was created. A year later Intel introduced the first microprocessor, and some forward-thinking engineers put away their slide rules in favor of a new invention—the pocket calculator. In 1981, IBM introduced the personal computer (PC), a tool that would forever change how people and computers co-exist—not only on the job, but also at home, at school, and even in the car. Six million PCs were sold in 1983, and in the world of business, fax machines went from being oddities to necessities. In 1984, Apple Macintosh introduced a novel, fun-to-use operating system that included graphics, icons, and an easy-to-hold pointing device known as a "mouse."

In 1985, IBM offered a computer-hungry public the 386 personal computer. To own one was to possess the greatest computer capacity yet devised for personal use. By 2000, the 386 chip was still around, but it no longer powered PCs. Today the chip is embedded into the paper numbers worn by marathon runners. At a race's start and finish lines, the chip interacts with an electronic beam to record the exact time each runner begins and ends the race. This once expensive, state-of-the-art chip is now cheap enough to discard at the race's end. Its swift journey from miracle to mundane poignantly captures the speed at which computers are evolving and the ways in which they have seamlessly infiltrated so many aspects of everyday life.

The Internet Spurs Computer Use

By the end of the 1980s, computers were clearly a part of every emerging communication technology. In 1988, about 4.7 million microcomputers and 120,000 minicomputers were sold in the United States.

One important ingredient in the rising popularity of personal computers was the Internet, a network most people readily associate with e-mail, or electronic messaging. The Internet, however, did not begin as a message service for the average citizen. Instead, researchers working for the U.S. Department of Defense in the late 1970s and early 1980s developed the Internet as a way to enable scientists at a handful of universities and government offices to share data from their high-speed computers.

But this network quickly blossomed into a personal communication tool, for the scientists quickly saw the network's potential as an electronic post office. They enjoyed sending each other comments about the latest science fiction novel or what they were going to do over the weekend, and this personal news traveled the network along with research findings. In 1984, the National Science Foundation provided funds for more government agencies and universities to expand the network and to improve it. Other groups, including private organizations, tapped into this growing network. By the late 1980s, the network was operating independently of the government and had become known as the "Internet."

By 2000, this global system linked more than 100 countries and had more than 200 million users, with 80 million in the United States. About seven new people go on the Internet every second, according to Cisco Systems, Inc., the world's largest Internet commerce site. Many are drawn to the Internet because they want the ease of communicating through e-mail. In fact, many people bought their first home computer so that they could send and receive e-mails.

In April 1999, when computer scientist and "Father of the Internet" Vinton G. Cerf spoke at a program called Computers, Freedom and Privacy, the number of people using the Internet had doubled every year since 1988. Cerf predicted that by 2006, "The Internet is likely to exceed the size of the global telephone network." By 2047, he ventured, "The world's population may reach about 11 billion. If only 25 percent of the then-world's population is on the Internet, that is nearly three billion users or ten times the population estimated at the end of [2000]." According to Cerf, the Internet's amazing growth could even reach to outer space: "Already interplanetary Internet is part of the NASA Mars mission program now under way at the Jet Propulsion Laboratory. By 2008, we should have a well-functioning Earth-Mars network that serves as a nascent backbone of an interplanetary systems of Internets."

The World Wide Web Is Born

The Internet's phenomenal growth and global reach has been spurred by the World Wide Web. Tim Berners-Lee, a London-born physicist, conceived of the Web in the late 1980s while working at CERN (the European Laboratory for Particle Physics) in Geneva, Switzerland. Working with colleagues, he designed the four essential elements that made the World Wide Web possible.

First, he developed the computer language that would code documents so they could be viewed on the Web. The language is known as HTML, or hypertext markup language. He also created the system, or protocol, that used the Internet to link documents together, no matter where they were located and regardless of whether they included text, graphics, or sound. This protocol is known as HTTP, or hypertext transfer protocol. The letters "http" now appear in most Web addresses. Berners-Lee also created the Web address system for documents, which is known as the universal resource locator, or URL. Every document must have a unique URL before it can be accessed via the Web.

But documents carrying HTML coding, using an HTTP protocol, and having a URL would be inaccessible without the software that could read the codes and addresses and retrieve the information. So, Berners-Lee also created the first browser program. He then gave the software away to anyone who wanted to download it, because he believed the Web must be available to everyone, free of charge.

In practical terms, this is how his system works. A student in India, for example, can go online and enter the Web address, or URL, for the *Encyclopedia Britannica*, which operates in Britain. If the student wants information on the Dutch postimpressionist painter Vincent Van Gogh, the student can type the painter's name into the Web site's search mechanism. The encyclopedia then offers its own page on Van Gogh and also provides links to other computers with information about the painter. With a click of the mouse, the student can connect to a virtual art gallery in Denver; a complete online catalogue located in Canada that shows all the artist's work; the archives of *USA Today*, which includes a newspaper article on Van Gogh; and numerous other sites.

The Web Will Change the World

Berners-Lee's vision brought the information of the world to every computer's doorstep. Some think the Web may impact today's society and culture as powerfully as Johann Gutenberg's printing press shook up fifteenth-century Europe. In fact, people believe Berners-Lee's invention, like Gutenberg's, will revolutionize the world. "I wouldn't be surprised if history records Tim Berners-Lee as the second Gutenberg . . . Gutenberg 2.0," said Jeffrey Bezos, founder and chief executive of Amazon.com, the Seattle-based online distributor of books and music, which has greatly profited from the Web's existence.

Life certainly was not the same after Gutenberg's press made it possible to mass produce books. Monks no longer had to laboriously hand-copy the few precious books that existed. As books became more plentiful, greater numbers of people were able to learn and share more ideas and use that knowledge to reshape their world. Many believe the worldwide linking of ideas via the Web also will forever change how people learn. Computers and the Internet have expanded the options of whom people can communicate with and when. They have made instant information the norm on the job, in the classroom, and at home. No wonder people refer to this time in history as the Information Revolution or the Information Age.

The Internet and the Web made the Information Revolution possible because those who created these tools wanted them to be free and open to all—a revolutionary idea. The Internet and the Web have the power to revolutionize society and culture precisely because of their democratic nature. They bring together people who otherwise may never have communicated with each other. When people go online to get e-mail or to surf the Web, they rarely notice the age, gender, race, geographic address, religious practice, or sexual orientation of those with whom they communicate. As long as they have access to the Internet, they can get information regardless of where they live, who they are, or what governments are in power.

Transforming Society and Culture

Clearly then, computers, the Internet, and the Web have transformed the way people live. The articles in this book explore those cultural and social areas where changes already have occurred. For example, computers and the Internet have transformed how people chat with friends, look for a job, share religious beliefs, or even find a date for Saturday night. Computer technology has transformed the business world. The Web has given birth to "e-commerce," the electronic exchange of goods and services. No one in sales can ignore the fact that in 2000, consumers spent almost $40 billion shopping online.

Popular entertainment has also been transformed—in some cases dramatically. It is now possible for people to download books and music directly from the Internet, and downloadable movies are on the horizon. In movie theaters viewers watch computer-generated films, with special effects that would have been unimaginable a decade ago. And while the movies incorporate computer technology, video games are looking more and more like interactive movies that present a "virtual reality" to an audience.

However, the Information Revolution also has also brought changes that people do not necessarily welcome. Indeed, the rapid pace of technology has raised some troubling issues, which several of the essays in this volume address. Many people, for example, are concerned that an open and instant flow of information will jeopardize their privacy or bring information to their home computers that they do not want their children to see. Others wonder how and when some governments might try to censor the Web or control access to it. Some researchers question whether constant Internet use will replace real human contact and make people feel more isolated. Still others note that people living in poverty or in rural areas are being left out of the Information Revolution.

The Future of Information Technology

In truth, no one knows how quickly or easily people will adapt to these social and cultural changes or where this ever-growing computer and Internet capability eventually will lead. Just as the people living in the late eighteenth century could not have predicted the full impact of the Industrial Revolution, people at the dawn of the twenty-first century cannot fully know how the Information Revolution will change the future. Because technology changes so quickly, it is not possible to predict life even ten years down the road.

Nevertheless, the selections in this volume point to areas where changes are definitely occurring, and the authors of these selections offer their insight into the future of information technology. Some computer scientists, for example, look to a time when homes come equipped with robots, or when books are read off of computer screens rather than paper. They believe that these developments will, like electricity, eventually become accepted as a normal part of everyday life. While some of the predictions about information technology seem far-fetched, Rich Karlgaard of *Forbes* notes that throughout modern history people have continually embraced ever-smarter machines. "People said no one will use answering machines or cell phones," he writes, "at first, people are slow to use them, then they do."

Examining Computers and the Internet

Today, if all the world's computers were to suddenly stop, life as people know it also would stop. The articles in *Examining Pop Culture: Computers and the Internet* give readers an insight into understanding how inextricably the technological age has been woven into their own lives. Essays in this volume examine five areas: the history of computers and the Internet; the ways in which they have transformed people's lives; their affect on popular entertainment; the potential problems they have wrought; and the future of information technology. The book reinforces the idea that a society touched by communication and information—whether in the time of Gutenberg or Berners-Lee—will be changed forever.

EXAMINING *POP* CULTURE

The Dawn
of the
Information Age

A Brief History of Computers

Jones Telecommunications and Multimedia Encyclopedia

Powered by steam and as large as a locomotive, the computer proposed by the English mathematician Charles Babbage in the 1820s would have looked nothing like today's computers. But it would have stored a computation program, calculated equations, and printed out the results. It was not until the 1940s and '50s that modern computers were born. Still large—one model was half the size of a football field—with miles of wires and thousands of vacuum tubes, these high-priced machines calculated at rapid speeds; but only the U.S. government could afford them. By the 1970s, computers had shrunk both in size and price. By the early 1980s, ordinary people were buying personal computers—or PCs—for their homes, schools, and offices. Now small enough to fit in a briefcase or in the palm of a hand, computers are much more than sophisticated calculators. They have become the essential tools of the Information Age. This brief history from the *Jones Telecommunications and Multimedia Encyclopedia*—an on-line reference— tells the story of these machines and their inventors.

THE REAL BEGINNINGS OF COMPUTERS AS WE know them today . . . lay with an English mathematics professor, Charles Babbage (1791–1871). Frustrated at the many errors he found while examining calculations for the Royal As-

■

tronomical Society, Babbage declared, "I wish to God these calculations had been performed by steam!" With those words,
the automation of computers had begun. By 1812, Babbage noticed a natural harmony between machines and mathematics:
machines were best at performing tasks repeatedly without mis-
take; while mathematics, particularly the production of mathe-
matic tables, often required the simple repetition of steps. The
problem centered on applying the ability of machines to the
needs of mathematics. Babbage's first attempt at solving this
problem was in 1822 when he proposed a machine to perform
differential equations, called a Difference Engine. Powered by
steam and large as a locomotive, the machine would have a
stored program and could perform calculations and print the
results automatically. After working on the Difference Engine
for 10 years, Babbage was suddenly inspired to begin work on
the first general-purpose computer, which he called the Analytical Engine. Babbage's assistant, Augusta Ada King, Countess of
Lovelace (1815–1842) and daughter of English poet Lord By-
ron, was instrumental in the machine's design. One of the few
people who understood the Engine's design as well as Babbage,
she helped revise plans, secure funding from the British government, and communicate the specifics of the Analytical Engine to the public. Also, Lady Lovelace's fine understanding of
the machine allowed her to create the instruction routines to be
fed into the computer, making her the first female computer
programmer. In the 1980's, the U.S. Defense Department
named a programming language ADA in her honor.

Babbage's steam-powered Engine, although ultimately
never constructed, may seem primitive by today's standards.
However, it outlined the basic elements of a modern general
purpose computer and was a breakthrough concept. Consisting of over 50,000 components, the basic design of the Analytical Engine included input devices in the form of perforated
cards containing operating instructions and a "store" for
memory of 1,000 numbers of up to 50 decimal digits long. It
also contained a "mill" with a control unit that allowed processing instructions in any sequence, and output devices to
produce printed results. Babbage borrowed the idea of punch
cards to encode the machine's instructions from the Jacquard
loom. The loom, produced in 1820 and named after its inven-

tor, Joseph-Marie Jacquard, used punched boards that controlled the patterns to be woven.

Punch Card Computers

In 1889, an American inventor, Herman Hollerith (1860–1929), also applied the Jacquard loom concept to computing. His first task was to find a faster way to compute the U.S. census. The previous census in 1880 had taken nearly seven years to count and with an expanding population, the bureau feared it would take 10 years to count the latest census. Unlike Babbage's idea of using perforated cards to instruct the machine, Hollerith's method used cards to store data information which he fed into a machine that compiled the results mechanically. Each punch on a card represented one number, and combinations of two punches represented one letter. As many as 80 variables could be stored on a single card. Instead of ten years, census takers compiled their results in just six weeks with Hollerith's machine. In addition to their speed, the punch cards served as a storage method for data and they helped reduce computational errors. Hollerith brought his punch card reader into the business world, founding Tabulating Machine Company in 1896, later to become International Business Machines (IBM) in 1924 after a series of mergers. Other companies such as Remington Rand and Burroughs also manufactured punch readers for business use. Both business and government used punch cards for data processing until the 1960's.

In the ensuing years, several engineers made other significant advances. Vannevar Bush (1890–1974) developed a calculator for solving differential equations in 1931. The machine could solve complex differential equations that had long left scientists and mathematicians baffled. The machine was cumbersome because hundreds of gears and shafts were required to represent numbers and their various relationships to each other. To eliminate this bulkiness, John V. Atanasoff (b. 1903), a professor at Iowa State College (now called Iowa State University) and his graduate student, Clifford Berry, envisioned an all-electronic computer that applied Boolean algebra to computer circuitry. This approach was based on the mid–19th century work of George Boole (1815–1864) who clarified the binary system of algebra, which stated that any mathematical equations could be stated simply as either true or false. By extending this concept to electronic circuits in the form of on or off, Atanasoff and Berry had developed the first all-electronic computer by 1940. Their project, however, lost its funding and their work was overshadowed by similar developments by other scientists.

First Generation Computers (1945–1956)

With the onset of the Second World War, governments sought to develop computers to exploit their potential strategic importance. This increased funding for computer development projects hastened technical progress. By 1941 German engineer Konrad Zuse had developed a computer, the Z3, to design airplanes and missiles. The Allied forces, however, made greater strides in developing powerful computers. In 1943, the British completed a secret code-breaking computer called Colossus to decode German messages. The Colossus's impact on the development of the computer industry was rather limited for two important reasons. First, Colossus was not a general-purpose computer; it was only designed to decode secret messages. Second, the existence of the machine was kept secret until decades after the war.

American efforts produced a broader achievement. Howard H. Aiken (1900–1973), a Harvard engineer working with IBM, succeeded in producing an all-electronic calculator by 1944. The purpose of the computer was to create ballistic charts for the U.S. Navy. It was about half as long as a football field and contained about 500 miles of wiring. The Harvard-IBM Automatic Sequence Controlled Calculator, or Mark I for short, was an electronic relay computer. It used electromagnetic signals to move mechanical parts. The machine was slow (taking 3–5 seconds per calculation) and inflexible (in that sequences of calculations could not change); but it could perform basic arithmetic as well as more complex equations.

Another computer development spurred by the war was the Electronic Numerical Integrator and Computer (ENIAC), produced by a partnership between the U.S. government and the University of Pennsylvania. Consisting of 18,000 vacuum tubes, 70,000 resistors and 5 million soldered joints, the computer was such a massive piece of machinery that it consumed

160 kilowatts of electrical power, enough energy to dim the lights in an entire section of Philadelphia. Developed by John Presper Eckert (1919–1995) and John W. Mauchly (1907–1980), ENIAC, unlike the Colossus and Mark I, was a general-purpose computer that computed at speeds 1,000 times faster than Mark I.

Breakthrough Advances

In the mid-1940's John von Neumann (1903–1957) joined the University of Pennsylvania team, initiating concepts in computer design that remained central to computer engineering for the next 40 years. Von Neumann designed the Electronic Discrete Variable Automatic Computer (EDVAC) in 1945 with a memory to hold both a stored program as well as data. This "stored memory" technique as well as the "conditional control transfer," that allowed the computer to be stopped at any point and then resumed, allowed for greater versatility in computer programming. The key element to the von Neumann architecture was the central processing unit, which allowed all computer functions to be coordinated through a single source. In 1951, the UNIVAC I (Universal Automatic Computer), built by Remington Rand, became one of the first commercially available computers to take advantage of these advances. Both the U.S. Census Bureau and General Electric owned UNIVACs. One of UNIVAC's impressive early achievements was predicting the winner of the 1952 presidential election, Dwight D. Eisenhower. . . .

Second Generation Computers (1956–1963)

By 1948, the invention of the transistor greatly changed the computer's development. The transistor replaced the large, cumbersome vacuum tube in televisions, radios and computers. As a result, the size of electronic machinery has been shrinking ever since. The transistor was at work in the computer by 1956. Coupled with early advances in magnetic-core memory, transistors led to second generation computers that were smaller, faster, more reliable and more energy-efficient than their predecessors. The first large-scale machines to take advantage of this transistor technology were early supercomputers, Stretch by IBM and LARC by Sperry-Rand. These computers, both developed for atomic energy laboratories, could handle an enormous amount of data, a capability much in demand by atomic scientists. The machines were costly, however, and tended to be too powerful for the business sector's computing needs, thereby limiting their attractiveness. Only two LARCs were ever installed: one in the Lawrence Radiation Labs in Livermore, California, for which the computer was named (Livermore Atomic Research Computer) and the other at the U.S. Navy Research and Development Center in Washington, D.C. Second generation computers replaced machine language with assembly language, allowing abbreviated programming codes to replace long, difficult binary codes.

Computers for Business Use

Throughout the early 1960's, there were a number of commercially successful second generation computers used in business, universities, and government from companies such as Burroughs, Control Data, Honeywell, IBM, Sperry-Rand, and others. These second generation computers were also of solid state design, and contained transistors in place of vacuum tubes. They also contained all the components we associate with the modern day computer: printers, tape storage, disk storage, memory, operating systems, and stored programs. One important example was the IBM 1401, which was universally accepted throughout industry, and is considered by many to be the Model T of the computer industry. By 1965, most large business routinely processed financial information using second generation computers.

It was the stored program and programming language that gave computers the flexibility to finally be cost effective and productive for business use. The stored program concept meant that instructions to run a computer for a specific function (known as a program) were held inside the computer's memory, and could quickly be replaced by a different set of instructions for a different function. A computer could print customer invoices and minutes later design products or calculate paychecks. More sophisticated high-level languages such as COBOL (Common Business-Oriented Language) and FORTRAN (Formula Translator) came into common use during this time, and have expanded to the current day. These languages replaced cryptic binary machine code with words, sentences, and mathematical formulas, making it much easier to program a computer. New types of careers (programmer, analyst, and computer systems expert) and the entire software industry began with second generation computers.

Third Generation Computers (1964–1971)

Though transistors were clearly an improvement over the vacuum tube, they still generated a great deal of heat, which damaged the computer's sensitive internal parts. The quartz rock eliminated this problem. Jack Kilby, an engineer with Texas Instruments, developed the integrated circuit (IC) in 1958. The IC combined three electronic components onto a small silicon disc, which was made from quartz. Scientists later managed to fit even more components on a single chip, called a semiconductor. As a result, computers became ever smaller as more components were squeezed onto the chip. Another third-generation development included the use of an operating system that allowed machines to run many different programs at once with a central program that monitored and coordinated the computer's memory.

Fourth Generation Computers (1971–Present)

After the integrated circuits, the only place to go was down—in size, that is. Large scale integration (LSI) could fit hundreds of components onto one chip. By the 1980's, very large scale integration (VLSI) squeezed hundreds of thousands of components onto a chip. Ultra-large scale integration (ULSI) increased that number into the millions. The ability to fit so much onto an area about half the size of a U.S. dime helped diminish the size and price of computers. It also increased their power, efficiency and reliability. The Intel 4004 chip, developed in 1971, took the integrated circuit one step further by locating all the components of a computer (central processing unit, memory, and input and output controls) on a minuscule chip. Whereas previously the integrated circuit had had to be manufactured to fit a special purpose, now one microprocessor could be manufactured and then programmed to meet any number of demands. Soon everyday household items such as microwave ovens, television sets and automobiles with electronic fuel injection incorporated microprocessors.

Such condensed power allowed everyday people to harness a computer's power. They were no longer developed exclusively for large business or government contracts. By the mid–1970's, computer manufacturers sought to bring computers to general consumers. These minicomputers came complete with user-friendly software packages that offered even non-technical users an array of applications, most popularly word processing and spreadsheet programs. Pioneers in this field were Commodore, Radio Shack and Apple Computers. In the early 1980's, arcade video games such as Pac Man and home video game systems such as the Atari 2600 ignited consumer interest for more sophisticated, programmable home computers.

The Personal Computer

In 1981, IBM introduced its personal computer (PC) for use in the home, office and schools. The 1980's saw an expansion in computer use in all three arenas as clones of the IBM PC made the personal computer even more affordable. The number of personal computers in use more than doubled from 2 million in 1981 to 5.5 million in 1982. Ten years later, 65 million PCs were being used. Computers continued their trend toward a smaller size, working their way down from desktop to laptop computers (which could fit inside a briefcase) to palmtop (able to fit inside a breast pocket). In direct competition with IBM's PC was Apple's Macintosh line, introduced in 1984. Notable for its user-friendly design, the Macintosh offered an operating system that allowed users to move screen icons instead of typing instructions. Users controlled the screen cursor using a mouse, a device that mimicked the movement of one's hand on the computer screen.

As computers became more widespread in the workplace, new ways to harness their potential developed. As smaller computers became more powerful, they could be linked together, or networked, to share memory space, software, information and communicate with each other. As opposed to a mainframe computer, which was one powerful computer that shared time with many terminals for many applications, networked computers allowed individual computers to form electronic co-ops. Using either direct wiring, called a Local Area Network (LAN), or telephone lines, these networks could reach enormous proportions. A global web of computer circuitry, the Internet, for example, links computers worldwide into a single network of information. During the 1992 U.S. presidential election, vice-presidential candidate Al Gore promised to make the development of this so-called "information superhighway" an administrative priority. Though the possibilities envisioned by Gore and others for such a large network are often years (if not decades) away from realization, the most popular use today for computer networks such as the Internet is electronic mail, or E-mail, which allows users to type in a computer address and send messages through networked terminals across the office or across the world.

The Origins of the Internet

Bruce Sterling

Given how widespread the Internet is today, it is hard to imagine that the idea for it was only born in the 1960s. Science fiction novelist and magazine writer Bruce Sterling provides an interesting, historic overview of ARPANET—a network that was first designed as a message system that could be used during a nuclear war. But as he notes, it unexpectedly blossomed into a peaceful exchange of news and information. Excited about their ability to communicate with each other via computers, ARPANET's researchers sent each other not only work-related messages, but also personal news. Theirs were the first e-mails. As the number of personal computers grew in the 1980s, so did the number of people linked to the network that eventually became known as the Internet. The Internet now has more than 100 million users in the United States and Canada, adds an estimated 2 million more a month, and is projected to include 500 million users worldwide by 2003. Written in 1992, Sterling's history has some outdated statistics, but his account of the birth of the Internet remains remarkable.

[IN THE EARLY 1960s,] THE RAND CORPORATION, America's foremost Cold War think-tank, faced a strange strategic problem. How could the US authorities successfully communicate after a nuclear war?

■

Excerpted from "Short History of the Internet," by Bruce Sterling, *The Magazine of Fantasy and Science Fiction*, February 1993. Reprinted by permission of the author.

A Nuclear Attack–Proof Network

Postnuclear America would need a command-and-control network, linked from city to city, state to state, base to base. But no matter how thoroughly that network was armored or protected, its switches and wiring would always be vulnerable to the impact of atomic bombs. A nuclear attack would reduce any conceivable network to tatters.

And how would the network itself be commanded and controlled? Any central authority, any network central citadel, would be an obvious and immediate target for an enemy missile. The center of the network would be the very first place to go. RAND mulled over this grim puzzle in deep military secrecy, and arrived at a daring solution. The RAND proposal (the brainchild of RAND staffer Paul Baran) was made public in 1964. In the first place, the network would *have no central authority*. Furthermore, it would be *designed from the beginning to operate while in tatters*.

Creating a Blast-Proof Network

The principles were simple. The network itself would be assumed to be unreliable at all times. It would be designed from the get-go to transcend its own unreliability. All the nodes in the network would be equal in status to all other nodes, each node with its own authority to originate, pass, and receive messages. The messages themselves would be divided into packets, each packet separately addressed. Each packet would begin at some specified source node, and end at some other specified destination node. Each packet would wind its way through the network on an individual basis.

The particular route that the packet took would be unimportant. Only final results would count. Basically, the packet would be tossed like a hot potato from node to node to node, more or less in the direction of its destination, until it ended up in the proper place. If big pieces of the network had been blown away, that simply wouldn't matter; the packets would still stay airborne, lateralled wildly across the field by whatever nodes happened to survive. This rather haphazard delivery system might be "inefficient" in the usual sense (especially compared to, say, the telephone system)—but it would be extremely rugged.

The First Networks

During the '60s, this intriguing concept of a decentralized, blast-proof, packet-switching network was kicked around by RAND, the Massachusetts Institute of Technology (MIT) and the Unversity of California–Los Angeles (UCLA). The National Physical Laboratory in Great Britain set up the first test network on these principles in 1968. Shortly afterward, the Pentagon's Advanced Research Projects Agency (ARPA) decided to fund a larger, more ambitious project in the USA. The nodes of the network were to be high-speed supercomputers (or what passed for supercomputers at the time). These were rare and valuable machines, which were in real need of good solid networking, for the sake of national research-and-development projects.

In fall 1969, the first such node was installed in UCLA. By December 1969, there were four nodes on the infant network, which was named ARPANET, after its Pentagon sponsor. The four computers could transfer data on dedicated high-speed transmission lines. They could even be programmed remotely from the other nodes. Thanks to ARPANET, scientists and researchers could share one another's computer facilities by long-distance. This was a very handy service, for computer-time was precious in the early '70s. In 1971 there were fifteen nodes in ARPANET; by 1972, thirty-seven nodes. And it was good.

The Birth of E-mail

By the second year of operation, however, an odd fact became clear. ARPANET's users had warped the computer-sharing network into a dedicated, high-speed, federally subsidized electronic post-office. The main traffic on ARPANET was not long-distance computing. Instead, it was news and personal messages. Researchers were using ARPANET to collaborate on projects, to trade notes on work, and eventually, to downright gossip and schmooze. People had their own personal user accounts on the ARPANET computers, and their own personal addresses for electronic mail. Not only were they using ARPANET for person-to-person communication, but they were very enthusiastic about this particular service—far more enthusiastic than they were about long-distance computation.

It wasn't long before the invention of the mailing-list, an ARPANET broadcasting technique in which an identical message could be sent automatically to large numbers of network subscribers. Interestingly, one of the first really big mailing-lists was "SF-LOVERS," for science fiction fans. Discussing science fiction on the network was not work-related and was frowned upon by many ARPANET computer administrators, but this didn't stop it from happening.

Throughout the '70s, ARPA's network grew. Its decentralized structure made expansion easy. Unlike standard corporate computer networks, the ARPA network could accommodate many different kinds of machines. As long as individual machines could speak the packet-switching lingua franca of the new, anarchic network, their brand-names, and their content, and even their ownership, were irrelevant.

Creating the Technical Standards

The ARPA's original standard for communication was known as NCP, "Network Control Protocol," but as time passed and the technique advanced, NCP was superceded by a higher-level, more sophisticated standard known as TCP/IP. TCP, or "Transmission Control Protocol," converts messages into streams of packets at the source, then reassembles them back into messages at the destination. IP, or "Internet Protocol," handles the addressing, seeing to it that packets are routed across multiple nodes and even across multiple networks with multiple standards—not only ARPA's pioneering NCP standard, but others like [the network protocols] Ethernet, FDDI, and X.25.

As early as 1977, TCP/IP was being used by other networks to link to ARPANET. ARPANET itself remained fairly tightly controlled, at least until 1983, when its military segment broke off and became MILNET. But TCP/IP linked them all. And ARPANET itself, though it was growing, became a smaller and smaller neighborhood amid the vastly growing galaxy of other linked machines.

Free, Easy Connection

As the '70s and '80s advanced, many very different social groups found themselves in possession of powerful computers. It was fairly easy to link these computers to the growing network-of-networks. As the use of TCP/IP became more common, entire other networks fell into the digital embrace of the Internet, and messily adhered. Since the software called TCP/IP was public-domain, and the basic technology was decentralized and rather anarchic by its very nature, it was difficult to stop people from barging in and linking up somewhere-or-other. In point of fact, nobody *wanted* to stop them from joining this branching complex of networks, which came to be known as the "Internet."

Connecting to the Internet cost the taxpayer little or nothing, since each node was independent, and had to handle its own financing and its own technical requirements. The more, the merrier. Like the phone network, the computer network became steadily more valuable as it embraced larger and larger territories of people and resources.

A fax machine is only valuable if *everybody else* has a fax machine. Until they do, a fax machine is just a curiosity. ARPANET, too, was a curiosity for a while. Then computer-networking became an utter necessity.

In 1984 the National Science Foundation (NSF) got into the act, through its Office of Advanced Scientific Computing. The new NSFNET set a blistering pace for technical advancement, linking newer, faster, shinier supercomputers, through thicker, faster links, upgraded and expanded, again and again, in 1986, 1988, 1990. And other government agencies leapt in: National Aeronautics and Space Admministration (NASA), the National Institutes of Health, the Department of Energy, each of them maintaining a digital satrapy in the Internet confederation. . . .

ARPANET itself formally expired in 1989, a happy victim of its own overwhelming success. Its users scarcely noticed, for ARPANET's functions not only continued but steadily improved. The use of TCP/IP standards for computer networking is now global. In 1971, a mere twenty-one years ago, there were only four nodes in the ARPANET network. [As of 1992] there are tens of thousands of nodes in the Internet, scattered over forty-two countries, with more coming on-line every day. Three million, possibly four million people use this gigantic mother-of-all-computer-networks. . . .

The Internet Sees Spectacular Growth

The Internet's pace of growth in the early 1990s is spectacular, almost ferocious. It is spreading faster than cellular phones, faster than fax machines. Last year [1991] the Internet was growing at a rate of twenty percent a *month*. The number of "host" machines with direct connection to TCP/IP has been doubling every year since 1988. The Internet is moving out of its original base in military and research institutions, into elementary and high schools, as well as into public libraries and the commercial sector.

Why do people want to be "on the Internet"? One of the main reasons is simple freedom. The Internet is a rare example of a true, modern, functional anarchy. There is no "Internet Inc." There are no official censors, no bosses, no board of directors, no stockholders. In principle, any node can speak as a peer to any other node, as long as it obeys the rules of the TCP/IP protocols, which are strictly technical, not social or political. (There has been some struggle over commercial use of the Internet, but that situation is changing as businesses supply their own links.)

The Internet is also a bargain. The Internet as a whole, unlike the phone system, doesn't charge for long-distance service. And unlike most commercial computer networks, it doesn't charge for access time, either. In fact the "Internet" itself, which doesn't even officially exist as an entity, never "charges" for anything. Each group of people accessing the Internet is responsible for their own machine and their own section of line.

The Internet's Anarchy

The Internet's "anarchy" may seem strange or even unnatural, but it makes a certain deep and basic sense. It's rather like the "anarchy" of the English language. Nobody rents English, and nobody owns English. As an English-speaking person, it's up to you to learn how to speak English properly and make whatever use you please of it (though the government provides certain subsidies to help you learn to read and write a bit). Otherwise, everybody just sort of pitches in, and somehow the thing evolves on its own, and somehow turns out workable. And interesting. Fascinating, even. Though a lot of people earn their living from using and exploiting and teaching English, "English" as an institution is public property, a public good. Much the same goes for the Internet. Would English be improved if "The English Language, Inc." had a board of directors and a chief executive officer, or a President and a Congress? There'd probably be a lot fewer new words in English, and a lot fewer new ideas.

People on the Internet feel much the same way about their own institution. It's an institution that resists institutionalization. The Internet belongs to everyone and no one.

Still, its various interest groups all have a claim. Business people want the Internet put on a sounder financial footing. Government people want the Internet more fully regulated. Academics want it dedicated exclusively to scholarly research. Military people want it spy-proof and secure. And so on and so on.

All these sources of conflict remain in a stumbling balance today, and the Internet, so far, remains in a thrivingly anarchical condition. Once upon a time, the NSFnet's high-speed, high-capacity lines were known as the "Internet Backbone," and their owners could rather lord it over the rest of the Internet; but today there are "backbones" in Canada, Japan, and Europe, and even privately owned commercial Internet backbones specially created for carrying business traffic. Today, even privately owned desktop computers can become Internet nodes. You can carry one under your arm. Soon, perhaps, on your wrist.

But what does one *do* with the Internet? Four things, basically: mail, discussion groups, long-distance computing, and file transfers.

E-mail and Newsgroups

Internet mail is "e-mail," electronic mail, faster by several orders of magnitude than the US Mail, which is scornfully known by Internet regulars as "snailmail." Internet mail is somewhat like fax. It's electronic text. But you don't have to pay for it (at least not directly), and it's global in scope. E-mail can also send software and certain forms of compressed digital imagery. New forms of mail are in the works.

The discussion groups, or "newsgroups," are a world of their own. This world of news, debate and argument is generally known as "USENET." USENET is, in point of fact, quite different from the Internet. USENET is rather like an enormous billowing crowd of gossipy, news-hungry people, wandering in and through the Internet on their way to various private backyard barbecues. USENET is not so much a physical network as a set of social conventions. In any case, at the moment there are some 2,500 separate newsgroups on USENET, and their discussions generate about 7 million words of typed commentary every single day. [Webopaedia, the on-line encyclopedia for computer technology, notes that in fall 2000 the number of newsgroups had exceeded 14,000.] Naturally there is a vast amount of talk about computers on USENET, but the variety of subjects discussed is enormous, and it's growing larger all the time. USENET also distributes various free electronic journals and publications.

Both netnews and e-mail are very widely available, even outside the high-speed core of the Internet itself. News and e-mail are easily available over common phone-lines, from Internet fringe-realms like BITnet, UUCP and Fidonet. The last two Internet services, long-distance computing and file transfer, require what is known as "direct Internet access"—using TCP/IP.

Long-Distance Computing and File Transfers

Long-distance computing was an original inspiration for ARPANET and is still a very useful service, at least for some. Programmers can maintain accounts on distant, powerful computers, run programs there or write their own. Scientists can make use of powerful supercomputers a continent away. Libraries offer their electronic card catalogs for free search. Enormous CD-ROM catalogs are increasingly available through this service. And there are fantastic amounts of free software available.

File transfers allow Internet users to access remote machines and retrieve programs or text. Many Internet computers . . . allow any person to access them anonymously, and to simply copy their public files, free of charge. This is no small deal, since entire books can be transferred through direct Internet access in a matter of minutes. . . . Internet file-transfers are becoming a new form of publishing, in which the reader simply electronically copies the work on demand, in any quantity he or she wants, for free. New Internet programs, such as "archie," "gopher," and "WAIS," have been developed to catalog and explore these enormous archives of material.

The Future of the Internet

The headless, anarchic, million-limbed Internet is spreading like bread-mold. Any computer of sufficient power is a potential spore for the Internet, and today such computers sell for less than $2,000 and are in the hands of people all over the world. ARPA's network, designed to assure control of a ravaged society after a nuclear holocaust, has been superceded by its mutant child the Internet, which is thoroughly out of control, and spreading exponentially through the post–Cold War electronic global village. The spread of the Internet in the '90s resembles the spread of personal computing in the 1970s, though it is even faster and perhaps more important. More important, perhaps, because it may give those personal computers a means of cheap, easy storage and access that is truly planetary in scale. . . .

The real Internet of the future may bear very little resemblance to today's plans. Planning has never seemed to have much to do with the seething, fungal development of the Internet. After all, today's Internet bears little resemblance to those original grim plans for RAND's post-holocaust command grid. It's a fine and happy irony.

Tim Berners-Lee and the Development of the World Wide Web

Margie Semilof

In 1990 Tim Berners-Lee wrote the computer program for what he christened the "World Wide Web" while working in Geneva, Switzerland, at the European Particle Physics Laboratory—known by the acronym CERN. Two things consistently impress those who have worked with him and those who only have heard of him: that his mind was able to envision and create something as sweeping and world altering as the World Wide Web and that he has never sought to profit from his creation. As *Computer Reseller News* reporter Margie Semilof notes in this overview of Berners-Lee and his invention, many want to idolize him. But Berners-Lee avoids the public eye and continues to guide the Web and its developments through the World Wide Web Consortium, which he directs. He has been a member of the Massachusetts Institute of Technology's Lab for Computer Science since 1994 and remains a strong advocate for a freeflowing and open Web that is unrestrained by government or business.

TO MANY PEOPLE, THE INTERNET IS THE GRAPHical element called the World Wide Web. And for that re-

∎

markable invention, the world can tip its collective hat to Tim Berners-Lee, the Web's developer.

The Web's Leader and Supporter

Berners-Lee is still the leader and remains the biggest evangelist for the entire World Wide Web universe. And if the Internet is the platform for the pipe networks of the world, then it is the Web that is the platform for all the applications of the world.

In fact, the total dollars spent by consumers shopping online is expected to top $40 billion by the year 2002, according to Jupiter Communications, a New York–based market-research firm. And to many, Berners-Lee is the unsung hero who started it all.

He shuns the limelight, preferring to work quietly in academia. Yet his contribution changed nearly every business in the world and freed the Internet from being strictly the province of gearheads. In fact, many companies now owe their very existence to Berners-Lee's creation.

"I wouldn't be surprised if history records Tim Berners-Lee as the second Gutenberg . . . Gutenberg 2.0," said Jeffrey Bezos, founder and chief executive of Amazon.com, Seattle, which recorded approximately $148 million in online book and music sales last year.

Those who know Berners-Lee say it rankles him when occasional credit for developing the World Wide Web goes to Marc Andreessen of Netscape Communications Corp. and others who exploited the Web using Mosaic browser technology invented at the University of Illinois in the early 1990s.

Berners-Lee, a London native, graduated with a degree in physics in 1976 from the Queen's College at Oxford University, England. His first job after college was in engineering at Plessey Telecommunications Ltd., a U.K.-based maker of telecommunications equipment.

The Origins of the Web

In the late 1970s, Berners-Lee wrote software programs for D.G. Nash Ltd. He joined CERN, the European Particle Physics Laboratory, in 1980. At CERN he wrote a program for his personal use, named Enquire, that would later be the conceptual start of the World Wide Web. Enquire was a name from a book written in 1858 that inspired Berners-Lee: "Inquire Within: Anything You Want To Know."

The program was put on the Internet the following summer. Berners-Lee continued his work on the Web and created early specifications of universal resource locators, HTTP and HTML.

He joined the Massachusetts Institute of Technology's Lab for Computer Science in 1994 and formed the World Wide Web Consortium, where he continues to serve as its director.

Many of Berners-Lee's former co-workers, colleagues and admirers consider him to be perhaps the greatest of all the Internet pioneers because of his vision and his continued altruistic involvement with the Web.

Not for Profit

There is a long and growing list of people who have profited from the Web, but Berners-Lee's name is not among them. Berners-Lee is still a research scientist and, even though he is working on his first book, which is due out next year [*Weaving the Web*, 1999], he has made every effort to avoid becoming a religious figure in a world loaded with technology icons.

"He is clearly a wizard and it's to his credit that he did something but never tried to exploit it for his own gain," said William Schrader, chief executive of PSINet Inc., a Herndon, Virginia, internet service provider (ISP) and the founder of NYSERNet, the first regional network in New York State, which provides services to universities, governments and corporations.

Tony Rutkowski, principal at Next Generation Internet Associates, a Herndon-based consulting firm, and former president of the Internet Society, said he has known Berners-Lee from their days in Geneva when Berners-Lee was at CERN and Rutkowski was at the International Telecommunications Union. Berners-Lee and his wife enjoyed acting in a local theater group, called The Little Theater of Geneva, which was run by Rutkowski's wife, Rutkowski said.

For Berners-Lee, the arts go hand-in-hand with his role as the Web's inventor, Rutkowski said. "The Web is more than just a technology," he said. "It's an interface of real human beings who share aggregate knowledge. That's different from those who grok the pipes, who could care less about what this stuff is used for or its consequence to real human beings."

Berners-Lee's knack for lateral thinking was recalled by more old friends at CERN. Brian Carpenter, now an IBM Corp. engineer in Hursley, England, ran the systems software team for computer controls of CERN Proton Synchrotron in 1980 where he met Berners-Lee, an application programmer. Carpenter remembered the invention of Enquire, which he described as a project that Berners-Lee worked on in his spare time.

"It wasn't the Web since it all ran within one computer, but it was the germ of the idea," Carpenter said in an E-mail.

For some, one of Berners-Lee's more memorable spare time projects happened when his boss refused to buy terminals in the temporary "huts" where Berners-Lee and other contract programmers sat. Berners-Lee had made a dummy terminal out of cardboard, and it had a plastic sleeve in place of the screen where he could slide in sheets of paper to "display" screen images, Carpenter said.

The Dream Behind the Web

The dream behind the Web is of a common information space in which we communicate by sharing information. Its universality is essential: the fact that a hypertext link can point to anything, be it personal, local or global, be it draft or highly polished. There was a second part of the dream, too, dependent on the Web being so generally used that it became a realistic mirror (or in fact the primary embodiment) of the ways in which we work and play and socialize. That was that once the state of our interactions was on line, we could then use computers to help us analyse it, make sense of what we are doing, where we individually fit in, and how we can better work together.

Tim Berners-Lee, "The World Wide Web: A Very Short Personal History," May 7, 1998, www.w3.org/people/berners-lee.

"Whenever someone showed up in his office, Tim would be typing on his cardboard terminal," Carpenter said. "Sadly, even this wasn't enough to get his boss to pay for real terminals. But it certainly had shades of [the comic strip] 'Dilbert,' even back in 1980."

Many Have Honored Him

These days, the man gets more respect. Berners-Lee has earned many honors, including a Duddell Medal of the Institute of Physics in 1997, an honorary degree from the Parsons School of Design, New York, and Southampton University, both in 1996, and an Institute of Electrical and Electronics Engineers (IEEE) Computer Society Wallace McDowell Award.

And then there is one award that probably warms his inner artist. At an international World Wide Web conference in Paris two years ago [1996], Berners-Lee and CERN donated the original machines used to develop the Web to the Louvre Museum.

Now far away from his days as an amateur actor, Berners-Lee avoids the public eye and shuns interviews. At an electronic-commerce conference in Boston last August [1998], he delivered a keynote that provided some insight as to where he believes the Internet and the Web are headed.

Berners-Lee's view of what the Web should be is twofold—a place for fluid communication, and a tool for machines to analyze data to remove the monkey work out of information processing so humans can focus on being creative.

Regarding the involvement of government in the development of the Web and E-commerce, he said, "My feeling is that when you have something common to everyone, it has to be run by the people for the people in a democratic way."

Berners-Lee said he doubts the American government will censor anything on the Web, and that the Web will remain an open and free-flowing form of communication. Just as he hopes. Just as he planned.

EXAMINING POP CULTURE

Changing
the Way
People Live

The Unforeseen Explosion of E-Commerce

Peter F. Drucker

When it began in the late 1700s, the Industrial Revolution was first identified with the steam engine. No one at the time foresaw that the steam engine would give birth to the railroad, an invention that changed the world forever. Peter F. Drucker, a professor of social science and the author of more than thirty books, notes the similarities between the Industrial Revolution and today's counterpart, the Information Revolution. Just as the railroad was the life-altering surprise of the Industrial Revolution, the Internet's e-commerce is the unforeseen offshoot of the Information Revolution. Using the Internet to buy and sell, to advertise, and even to hire has dramatically changed the world of business and will continue to have a profound impact on the world economy.

THE TRULY REVOLUTIONARY IMPACT OF THE INformation Revolution is just beginning to be felt. But it is not "information" that fuels this impact. It is not "artificial intelligence." It is not the effect of computers and data processing on decision-making, policymaking, or strategy. It is something that practically no one foresaw or, indeed, even talked about ten or fifteen years ago: *e-commerce*—that is, the explosive emergence of the Internet as a major, perhaps eventually *the* major, worldwide distribution channel for goods, for services,

■

Excerpted from "Beyond the Revolution," by Peter F. Drucker, *The Atlantic Monthly*, October 1999. Reprinted by permission of the author.

and, surprisingly, for managerial and professional jobs. This is profoundly changing economies, markets, and industry structures; products and services and their flow; consumer segmentation, consumer values, and consumer behavior; jobs and labor markets. But the impact may be even greater on societies and politics and, above all, on the way we see the world and ourselves in it. . . .

It is likely that other new technologies will appear suddenly, leading to major new industries. What they may be is impossible even to guess at. But it is highly probable—indeed, nearly certain—that they will emerge, and fairly soon. And it is nearly certain that few of them—and few industries based on them—will come out of computer and information technology. Like biotechnology and fish farming, each will emerge from its own unique and unexpected technology.

Of course, these are only predictions. But they are made on the assumption that the Information Revolution will evolve as several earlier technology-based "revolutions" have evolved over the past 500 years, since Gutenberg's printing revolution, around 1455. In particular the assumption is that the Information Revolution will be like the Industrial Revolution of the late eighteenth and early nineteenth centuries. And that is indeed exactly how the Information Revolution has been during its first fifty years.

The Steam Engine and the Computer

The Information Revolution is now at the point at which the Industrial Revolution was in the early 1820s, about forty years after James Watt's improved steam engine (first installed in 1776) was first applied, in 1785, to an industrial operation— the spinning of cotton. And the steam engine was to the first Industrial Revolution what the computer has been to the Information Revolution—its trigger, but above all its symbol. Almost everybody today believes that nothing in economic history has ever moved as fast as, or had a greater impact than, the Information Revolution. But the Industrial Revolution moved at least as fast in the same time span, and had probably an equal impact if not a greater one. In short order it mechanized the great majority of manufacturing processes, beginning with the production of the most important industrial commodity of the eighteenth and early nineteenth centuries: textiles. [Gordon] Moore's Law [first observed in 1965] asserts that the price of the Information Revolution's basic element, the microchip, drops by 50 percent every eighteen months. The same was true of the products whose manufacture was mechanized by the first Industrial Revolution. The price of cotton textiles fell by 90 percent in the fifty years spanning the start of the eighteenth century. The production of cotton textiles increased at least 150-fold in Britain alone in the same period. And although textiles were the most visible product of its early years, the Industrial Revolution mechanized the production of practically all other major goods, such as paper, glass, leather, and bricks. . . .

[T]he Industrial Revolution in its first half century only mechanized the production of goods that had been in existence all along. It tremendously increased output and tremendously decreased cost. It created both consumers and consumer products. But the products themselves had been around all along. And products made in the new factories differed from traditional products only in that they were uniform, with fewer defects than existed in products made by any but the top craftsmen of earlier periods. . . .

The Revolutionary Railroad

Then, in 1829, came the railroad, a product truly without precedent, and it forever changed economy, society, and politics.

In retrospect it is difficult to imagine why the invention of the railroad took so long. Rails to move carts had been around in coal mines for a very long time. What could be more obvious than to put a steam engine on a cart to drive it, rather than have it pushed by people or pulled by horses? But the railroad did not emerge from the cart in the mines. It was developed quite independently. And it was not intended to carry freight. On the contrary, for a long time it was seen only as a way to carry people. Railroads became freight carriers thirty years later, in America. (In fact, as late as the 1870s and 1880s the British engineers who were hired to build the railroads of newly Westernized Japan designed them to carry passengers—and to this day Japanese railroads are not equipped to carry freight.) But until the first railroad actually began to operate, it was virtually unanticipated.

Within five years, however, the Western world was engulfed by the biggest boom history had ever seen—the railroad boom. Punctuated by the most spectacular busts in economic history, the boom continued in Europe for thirty years, until the late 1850s, by which time most of today's major railroads had been built. In the United States it continued for another thirty years, and in outlying areas—Argentina, Brazil, Asian Russia, China—until the First World War.

The railroad was the truly revolutionary element of the Industrial Revolution, for not only did it create a new economic dimension but also it rapidly changed what I would call the *mental geography*. For the first time in history human beings had true mobility. For the first time the horizons of ordinary people expanded. Contemporaries immediately realized that a fundamental change in mentality had occurred. (A good account of this can be found in what is surely the best portrayal of the Industrial Revolution's society in transition, George Eliot's 1871 novel *Middlemarch*.) . . .

Computers Simply Speed Up Processes

Like the Industrial Revolution two centuries ago, the Information Revolution so far—that is, since the first computers, in the mid–1940s—has only transformed processes that were here all along. In fact, the real impact of the Information Revolution has not been in the form of "information" at all. Almost none of the effects of information envisaged forty years ago have actually happened. For instance, there has been practically no change in the way major decisions are made in business or government. But the Information Revolution has routinized traditional *processes* in an untold number of areas.

The software for tuning a piano converts a process that traditionally took three hours into one that takes twenty minutes. There is software for payrolls, for inventory control, for delivery schedules, and for all the other routine processes of a business. Drawing the inside arrangements of a major building (heating, water supply, sewerage, and so on) such as a prison or a hospital formerly took, say, twenty-five highly skilled draftsmen up to fifty days; now there is a program that enables one draftsman to do the job in a couple of days, at a tiny fraction of the cost. There is software to help people do their tax returns and software that teaches hospital residents how to take out a gall bladder. The people who now speculate in the stock market online do exactly what their predecessors in the 1920s did while spending hours each day in a brokerage office. The processes have not been changed at all. They have been routinized, step by step, with a tremendous saving in time and, often, in cost.

The psychological impact of the Information Revolution, like that of the Industrial Revolution, has been enormous. It has perhaps been greatest on the way in which young children learn.

Teenage Entrepreneurs

Just as the average age of Internet users is going down, so is the average age of Internet entrepreneurs. But boys so far outnumber girls is this new business arena.

All the "elderly" Internet tycoons in their twenties and thirties had better watch out. The average age of the Internet entrepreneur will plummet over the next five years, according to research firm Computer Economics, as more kids take their business ideas to the Web.

"I can tell you that teens are so advanced when it comes to the Web that they can use it to successfully target peers. They know where other teens hang out and can market directly to them through chat groups and other online meeting places like gaming sites," says Chris Anne Wheeler, vice president of information services at research firm ActivMedia. Wheeler advises Web business veterans to look to the new teen entrepreneurs for lessons on how to take better advantage of online business opportunities.

In a survey of San Diego County high school seniors, Computer Economics also found that 8 percent of students already run online businesses, and 56 percent plan to start them.

Sharon Nash, *PC Magazine*, May 9, 2000.

Beginning at age four (and often earlier), children now rapidly develop computer skills, soon surpassing their elders; computers are their toys and their learning tools. Fifty years hence we may well conclude that there was no "crisis of American education" in the closing years of the twentieth century—there was only a growing incongruence between the way twentieth-century schools taught and the way late-twentieth-century children learned. Something similar happened in the sixteenth-century university, a hundred years after the invention of the printing press and movable type. . . .

E-Commerce Makes Geography Almost Irrelevant

E-commerce is to the Information Revolution what the railroad was to the Industrial Revolution—a totally new, totally unprecedented, totally unexpected development. And like the railroad 170 years ago, e-commerce is creating a new and distinct boom, rapidly changing the economy, society, and politics.

One example: A mid-sized company in America's industrial Midwest, founded in the 1920s and now run by the grandchildren of the founder, used to have some 60 percent of the market in inexpensive dinnerware for fast-food eateries, school and office cafeterias, and hospitals within a hundred-mile radius of its factory. China is heavy and breaks easily, so cheap china is traditionally sold within a small area. Almost overnight this company lost more than half of its market. One of its customers, a hospital cafeteria where someone went "surfing" on the Internet, discovered a European manufacturer that offered china of apparently better quality at a lower price and shipped cheaply by air. Within a few months the main customers in the area shifted to the European supplier. Few of them, it seems, realize—let alone care—that the stuff comes from Europe.

In the new mental geography created by the railroad, humanity mastered distance. In the mental geography of e-commerce, distance has been eliminated. There is only one economy and only one market.

One consequence of this is that every business must become globally competitive, even if it manufactures or sells only within a local or regional market. The competition is not local anymore—in fact, it knows no boundaries. Every company has to become transnational in the way it is run. Yet the traditional multinational may well become obsolete. It manufactures and distributes in a number of distinct geographies, in which it is a *local* company. But in e-commerce there are neither local companies nor distinct geographies. Where to manufacture, where to sell, and how to sell will remain important business decisions. But in another twenty years they may no longer determine what a company does, how it does it, and where it does it.

New Types of Businesses Will Emerge

At the same time, it is not yet clear what kinds of goods and services will be bought and sold through e-commerce and what kinds will turn out to be unsuitable for it. This has been true whenever a new distribution channel has arisen. . . .

Here are a few examples. Twenty-five years ago it was generally believed that within a few decades the printed word would be dispatched electronically to individual subscribers' computer screens. Subscribers would then either read text on their computer screens or download it and print it out. This was the assumption that underlay the CD-ROM. Thus any number of newspapers and magazines, by no means only in the United States, established themselves online; few, so far, have become gold mines. But anyone who twenty years ago predicted the business of Amazon.com and barnesandnoble.com— that is, that books would be sold on the Internet but delivered in their heavy, printed form—would have been laughed off the podium. Yet Amazon.com and barnesandnoble.com are in exactly that business, and they are in it worldwide. The first order for the U.S. edition of my most recent book, *Management Challenges for the 21st Century* (1999), came to Amazon.com, and it came from Argentina.

Changing How Customers Buy

Another example: Ten years ago one of the world's leading automobile companies made a thorough study of the expected impact on automobile sales of the then emerging Internet. It concluded that the Internet would become a major distribution channel for used cars, but that customers would still want to see new cars, to touch them, to test-drive them. In actuality, at least so far, most used cars are still being bought not over the Internet but in a dealer's lot. However, as many as half of all new cars sold (excluding luxury cars) may now actually be "bought" over the Internet. Dealers only deliver cars that customers have chosen well before they enter the dealership. What does this mean for the future of the local automobile dealership, the twentieth century's most profitable small business? . . .

This illustrates another important effect of e-commerce. New distribution channels change who the customers are. They change not only *how* customers buy but also *wha*t they buy. They change consumer behavior, savings patterns, industry structure—in short, the entire economy. This is what is now happening, and not only in the United States but increasingly in the rest of the developed world, and in a good many emerging countries, including mainland China.

Finding Love Online

Jill Sell

Cyberdating—meeting someone online—is growing in popularity among people too busy or too shy to obtain face-to-face dates. Many people consider Internet dating to be both risky and impersonal, but newspaper journalist Jill Sell, who writes for Cleveland's *The Plain Dealer*, reports that researchers have a more positive view of this modern way to meet and possibly court someone. Dating online, she notes, hearkens back to earlier times when letter writing was the principal way men and women shared their most personal feelings. Many online romances do not end with happily-ever-after stories. But a large number of people who enjoy writing as a way to share their thoughts and emotions are discovering that cyberdating can definitely broaden their romantic possibilities.

MOST PEOPLE WOULDN'T CONSIDER TOENAILS A romantic subject. But for Debbie Thorn, 39, of Cleveland, an online discussion about that subject helped her decide she'd found true love. More about that later.

Thorn met her first husband at WGAR, the Cleveland radio station where they both worked. The couple dated for 10 years, were married for four, and had a 2-year-old daughter named Samantha. All was right with the world—until her husband died after a heart attack in 1992.

Lonely and wanting to pick up the pieces of her life, Thorn joined Parents Without Partners, but found her schedule didn't

■

permit her to participate in many of the group's activities.

"They did things late at night like bowling at midnight," recalled Thorn. "What was I supposed to do with my 2-year-old daughter?"

So Thorn stayed home and did what millions of single Americans are doing—she went online to find friendship and romance. She would tuck Samantha in bed, kiss her good-night, turn on the computer and go on the Internet.

"Cyberdating will become more and more common just because people are so busy. It allows us to sort through more available people in a much quicker, easier way," said Andrea Baker, who is researching romance in cyberspace. "I have been surprised at how people are able to establish a relationship quite quickly, even just through e-mail, and how people seem to know when they meet that right person."

Cyber-Romances May Be More Honest

Baker, assistant professor of sociology at Ohio University's Lancaster campus, began her research in 1997 and now has data on 43 couples (most engaged, living together or married), ages 18 to 50. She believes romances formed online may be "better and deeper than many real-life meetings because these couples are honest with each other in their writings."

For many people in our culture, written communication had dwindled to signing your name on a birthday card. But according to Baker, the new technology has actually created "a respect for the power and finality of the written word that hasn't existed in generations."

Singles are looking for the person of their dreams through Web sites for dating services, chat rooms, e-mail and posted messages. Cupid is also lurking in online game rooms, as well as special interest sites, an option Baker especially likes because she believes potential matches start with common interests, whether that's bird-watching, sky diving or French literature.

Baker believes people, especially men, are "less shy and less introverted" when online than if meeting someone in person. Also, "physical appearances become distractions," and often couples are doing other things (such as having lunch in a restaurant) which can also interfere with getting to know someone, she said. The couples Baker has studied chatted online from weeks to years before they met in person.

For Thorn, it was a matter of months. She bought a computer in February 1996, met her future husband, Bill Thorn, in an online chat room in April, started talking to him by phone in July and met him face to face in September.

The couple married over Labor Day weekend in 1998. It might have even been sooner, but Bill Thorn, 39, lived in New Mexico.

"I was just lucky Debbie didn't live in Alaska," said Bill, who came to Ohio for the couple's first in-person meeting.

"Bill wanted me to meet him halfway the first time, but how could I do that with my daughter?" recalled Debbie. "And my parents would never go for me getting on a plane to meet a stranger. Bill knew the only way it was going to work was for him to come to Cleveland."

Bill, who had never been married, was "prepared to leave at a moment's notice if things didn't work out." Instead, he stayed a week. He believes "saying something online that made Debbie laugh" helped get her interested.

"And I guess I was different from a lot of people who are out there only looking to make a quick kill. I wasn't desperate. I didn't ask Debbie her measurements or what she was wearing like some kids online do. I wasn't in the chat rooms looking for a wife. It was late at night and I was lonely and I just wanted to have fun talking to people," said Bill, whose log-on name was Buzz-worm. "I wasn't out to make any lasting relationships, so I was relaxed. And we took our time and proceeded with caution."

Less Stress on Good Looks

Couples who meet online do place less emphasis on the physical, said Baker. Her "most successful" couples didn't exchange photographs until the relationship was well-established online or by phone.

"I even have one couple who didn't see pictures until they met for the first time, and they were both extremely attractive people," said Baker. "The woman, in particular, didn't want looks to be all that important. They were pleased with how each other looked, but they really wanted to communicate on the intellectual level."

Debbie (her log-on was Fine Lady) sent Bill "a glamour shot" and when he saw it, he asked if she "looked that way all the time."

"I said, yep, sure, even in the morning," said Debbie. "Bill sent me a picture where he wasn't smiling. But I kind of have this thing for nice teeth, so I asked him, 'So, do you have teeth?' He said, Yeah. One green one. Does it matter?' And it really didn't because at that time I had already fallen in love with him."

One of the reasons Debbie felt good about Bill was the fact that every Sunday he would drive to his grandmother's house 30 miles away and clip her toenails because it was something that was very important to her.

"How many men would give up a Sunday to do that? She also had a job jar waiting for him. I knew if he cared that much about his grandmother, he'd be good to me and my daughter, too," said Debbie.

The biggest step for Bill was moving to Ohio to be near Debbie. "I knew I had some marketable skills and could find a job in Ohio. Plus, my former employer said I could come back if things didn't work," said Bill, a technician for Honeywell in Strongsville. "I also had some money saved, and it's good to have a safety net if someone is thinking of doing something similar."

Change Is Easier for the Young

"In one sense, younger people have an advantage when meeting someone in cyberspace. They may not have a lot of money, but they have fewer responsibilities with family or work than older people. A younger person can just change colleges or a job if they meet someone online who is out of state," said Baker. "But on the other hand, an older person may have a lot of motivation to find someone and be willing to make big changes. Who does the moving? In older couples, it tends to be more traditional, and women tend to be the ones who move, but it can go either way."

Former Massillon resident Sara Freeman, 26, followed her heart to Austin, Texas, where she married Chris Freeman, 32, in 1997. A year before that, Sara was a college student at Kent State University's Stark County campus taking a computer class and just surfing a site for singles. The eye-catcher for

Sara was that Chris, a director of customer service for a company that secures online transactions, was a single father with a 4½-year-old son. She was single parenting a son, 3½, and a daughter, 1½.

Sara was the first to suggest the two exchange phone numbers ("that's when our phone bills went to $400 a month"), and that led to a photo exchange.

"When we met for the first time, I didn't recognize him at the airport because his photo was about three years old and he had gained 20 to 30 pounds. I walked right by him," recalled Sara. "After that meeting, though, we knew we were seriously interested in each other. But we also had to see how we reacted to each other's kids."

When Sara took her first trip to Texas, she "had everyone's phone number back home," and an aunt and uncle who promised to send her money if things were less than perfect.

"But I probably would never have agreed to meet Chris at all except for the fact that I had references. I was always talking to his best friend and his best friend's wife. But everything has worked out fine. I went from living paycheck to paycheck to a (big) house, two brand new cars and kids' activities up the kazoo."

Not Always the Answer

Those are the good stories, of course. For every happy couple, there are dozens of dead ends and false starts, said Baker. She does think it can be easier if someone has a flair for being online and "has some writing or communication skills." But she said people tend to find their matches on many different levels.

Others see cyberdating as a tool but not the ultimate answer for living happily ever after. Alka Gupta, who works for the search engine group Lycos, said the Internet is "not the end all, be all, and it won't replace romance as we know it today.

"It's like e-commerce and shopping. There will always be those who want to pick the apples themselves to make sure they're not too soft," said Gupta, who said searching the Web should be considered an augmentation to traditional dating. "But there are a lot of advantages to cyberdating, including lower phone bills."

Religion Online

Paul A. Soukup

Jesuit priest Paul A. Soukup notes that throughout history religious groups have quickly adapted the newest communication technologies for their own use. A professor of communication at Santa Clara University in California and the author of *Media, Culture and Catholicism*, Soukup points to the printing press, Hollywood's Biblical movies, radio and television programs that star evangelists, and now the Internet as examples of technological advances that have helped to spread religious messages even as they have brought change to religious institutions.

THAT RELIGION APPEARS ON THE INTERNET should not surprise anyone. After all, individuals and churches have quickly adopted almost every communication technology, beginning with Johannes Gutenberg's printing press, which turned out the Bible as its first product.

Closer to this century, we saw a fledgling motion picture industry produce Bible films and biblical epics, satisfying both piety and box-office demand. Two films based on the passion of Christ appeared in 1897: *Lear Passion* (France) and *The Horitz Passion Play* (United States, but filmed in Bohemia). The next 20 years saw other passion plays, lives of Christ and epics like the Judean episode of [filmmaker] D.W. Griffith's *Intolerance* (1916). Cecil B. DeMille made a career of the entertaining biblical drama: *The Ten Commandments* (1923), *The King of Kings* (1927), *The Sign of the Cross* (1932), all the way to the remake of *The Ten Commandments* (1956). Religious and biblical films form a cinematic tradition that continues to this day.

■

Religious Radio and Television

Something similar happened with radio. Within its first months of operation, KDKA, Frank Conrad's pioneering Pittsburgh radio station [first commercial station], went on location to the Calvary Episcopal Church, where a precociously ecumenical crew of engineers donned choir robes to broadcast the sermon. This first effort opened the doors to religious broadcasting of all kinds: the evangelism of Aimee Semple McPherson [a controversial U.S. Pentecostal preacher], the social preaching of Father Charles Coughlin [a Roman Catholic "radio priest" of the 1930s], the "Old Fashioned Revival Hour" of Charles Fuller, the "Sacred Heart Program" of Father Eugene Murphy and even the wildly popular but ultimately doomed on-air denunciations of Los Angeles sinners by Robert "Fighting Bob" Shuler in the 1920s. Religious radio survives in a more mature form, of course, in almost every city and stretch of lonely highway, featuring sermons, Bible study, prayer, talk and music.

Broadcast television, too, had its early religious moments. Who can forget Bishop Fulton Sheen giving [comedian] Milton Berle a run for the ratings with his "Life Is Worth Living" series? The Rev. Billy Graham's crusades drew huge local and national television audiences. Though network coverage of religious topics has fallen off now that the FCC [Federal Communications Commission] no longer requires that they offer free time to religious groups, the networks still regularly carry the papal Christmas Mass and other religious services.

Cable television and its satellite distribution proved an even more fertile ground for religious television. The evangelical churches have taken the lead by creating imaginative programming like the "700 Club" and the "P.T.L. Club," or producing televangelists like Oral Roberts, Pat Robertson, Jerry Falwell, Robert Schuller, Jim and Tammy Bakker, and Jimmy Swaggart. In the Catholic tradition, Mother Angelica has successfully maintained a cable network, EWTN, and an ecumenical group launched the Faith and Values (now Odyssey) network.

With a heritage like this, the Internet seems assured of religious use.

Technology Spreads the Message

That heritage endures because it has a theoretical backup. The rapid adoption of new communication technologies by the Christian churches stems from a number of factors. The centrality and importance of the Bible guarantees content for Christian programming and an initial audience. A generally optimistic view of technology (what the Second Vatican Council called "the marvelous technical inventions" of the modern age) leads to a willingness to try new tools. And the felt urgency of the Great Commission ("Go, therefore, make disciples of all the nations, baptizing them in the name of the Father, and of the Son, and of the Holy Spirit"—Mt. 28:19) motivates individuals and churches to do whatever they can to spread the good news. Ben Armstrong of the National Religious Broadcasters claims that reflecting on that passage of Matthew's Gospel led directly to the evangelical use of broadcast satellites. Paul VI made a similar point: "The church would feel itself guilty before God if it did not avail itself of those powerful instruments which human skill is constantly developing and perfecting. With their aid it may preach 'upon the housetops' the message which has been entrusted to it" (*Evangelii Nuntiandi*, [The Gospel must be proclaimed] No. 45).

What Is On-Line?

If Christians naturally use new technologies, then the Internet provides an opportunity to see how they use them. Just what is out there on-line? A quick look at the World Wide Web using a standard search engine shows 16,500 "faiths and practices" sites and 12,000 "Christianity" sites. These include 970 churches, of which 360 are Catholic parishes. Catholic institutions are well represented: 125 religious order sites, over 100 religious publications and 130 other Catholic organizations. Over 150 seminary Web pages appear, of which Catholic seminaries sponsor 12.

The Vatican has its own Web site, complete with texts of recent documents. The National Conference of Catholic Bishops and the United States Catholic Conference also have a site, as do about two-thirds of the dioceses in the United States.

The Bible appears on at least 250 sites, with another 10

devoted to selling Bible software. Homiletics is popular, with over 1,000 sites, some containing homily hints; many others present the homilies of individual pastors.

The Web also contains archives of ecclesiastical and theological documents from a variety of Christian traditions, plus links to a dozen theological libraries. These usually contain still more links to religious references around the world.

Web indices list spirituality sites from angels to women's spirituality.

What's on-line in religion? A quick synthetic summary would include reference materials (the Bible, theological texts, homilies and homiletic resources, religious documents), institutional information (dioceses, churches, religious communities, publications), spirituality (Bible study, meditation guides, spiritual advice) and evangelism (apologetics, catechetical information, personal witness).

How Is the Internet Being Used?

Though such richness delights the imagination, on-line religion raises a number of questions for further reflection, most with no easy answers.

A difficult but not impossible question arises when we ask how people use religious resources on the Internet. I honestly don't think anyone has done any empirical research on the question, but judging from what is known of other religious communication, I will guess that the use falls into five broad categories. First, people find on-line religion a good reference tool for locating churches, church organizations and documents. Second, it serves a study or educational need: People can learn from its content. Third, some on-line religious material provides the high-tech equivalent of spiritual reading. It nourishes and lifts the spirit in a contemporary and interactive way. Fourth, on-line religion can foster a kind of community—at least a virtual community—with like-minded individuals. Indeed, a number of sites encourage a more conscious community through chat rooms and bulletin board discussions. And, fifth, those Internet sites both confirm and validate people who see their beliefs, churches, organizations, pastors, schools and so forth on line.

A second important question (and one also open to research) asks who has provided all this religious material. As the now famous Steiner cartoon in *The New Yorker* put it—the dog at the computer keyboard talking to the other dog—"On the Internet, no one knows you're a dog." Religious Internet sites, like every Internet site, have no verification, and every page looks equally credible. A search for "Catholic teachings" could equally well turn up the Vatican Web site, that of a fourth grade C.C.D. [Confraternity of Christian Doctrine] class and one from a group opposed to Catholic thought. As a popular medium, the Internet does not have (and generally opposes) editorial control or editorial review.

Many see the anonymity and openness of the Internet as a virtue; it promotes more active participation and provides an equally high soapbox to every person. If "no one knows you're a dog," then no one can judge you except on the merits of your ideas, goes the received wisdom.

What Is Not Represented?

Lest we get lost in a kind of populist admiration for the Internet, we should also ask a third question: "Who is not there?" or "What is not represented?" These questions apply just as much to religious content as to other content; we must recognize that the Internet currently excludes as many voices as it promotes. Those without access to technology do not appear on the Internet. That category includes people already marginalized, people with low incomes, people of certain educational levels, people with some hesitation about technology and people busy with other things. The Gospel poor, by and large, do not share in on-line religion as we now see it. Even without gatekeepers, the Internet has its gates.

Other questions appear in this context of larger issues. Despite the sense of virtual community, what does on-line religion do to religious experience? Does it privatize practice more than other religious technologies and practices? Or does it involve people more in religious expression? Can on-line religion evangelize? The evidence here appears mixed. Just as with other newer communication technologies (television and cable television, for example), the technology isolates some people, highlighting the individualistic aspects of religion, while bringing other people more actively into a Christian community. No technology affects everyone in the same way.

What Difference Will It Make?

Finally, does all this matter? In a word, yes—and not just in terms of who uses the Internet, who does not, and how they do or do not use it. It is possible that the church will be vastly transformed by information. The Internet provides immediate access to a wide range of religious materials, usually more quickly than do the traditional channels of distribution. For example, Pope John Paul's encyclical *Fides et Ratio* [Faith and Reason] appeared on the Vatican Web site the same day the Vatican released the text. This allowed people throughout the world to bypass commentators and news reports and read it for themselves.

The Internet also has the potential to increase the number and range of voices participating in religious discussions. The pope and the bishops do not hold a monopoly on religious Web sites. In fact, this phenomenon of open discussion of religious issues, free of the control of church bodies and freely available to large numbers of people, introduces something quite new into the church and into theology. Since discussions can no longer remain strictly "in house," the Internet promotes a kind of grass-roots ecumenism and interreligious dialogue. When the Second Vatican Council called for greater information and public opinion in the church, few if any participants envisioned opening the windows quite so widely, much less did they foresee Windows 95.

Technology Affects Religious Practice

Each new communication technology and its rapid adoption has introduced a new context that affects religious practice. The printed Bible made it possible for everyone to own a Bible, to read it and to study it. In the Reformers' vision, it made possible unmediated access to the word of God.

The mass media of radio, television and film intensified the communication process and allowed instantaneous (and mostly one-way) information to reach great numbers of people. By their very nature, however, radio, television and film heightened centralized control and one-to-many transmission and in the process made people more aware of and a bit suspicious of centralization and hierarchy. By fostering entertainment and spectacle, they reintroduced the visual pageantry the Reformers had removed.

The Internet is the first communication technology with the possibility of many-to-many communication, and with the possibility of a true democratizing of communication. It is too early to predict where this will lead, but it is safe to conclude that it will have religious consequences no less profound than those brought about by the older communication technologies.

Teenagers Make Instant Messaging a Hot Idea

Chris Wood

Instant messaging (IM) programs are seen as a hot growth area for Internet companies like Yahoo! and America Online. Faster, chattier, and more casual than e-mail, instant messaging is particularly popular among teenagers. Friends who list each other on their "buddy lists" can carry on simultaneous e-mail conversations with everyone who is logged on from their group. Teenage girls are the largest group of IM users, but the benefits of IM have not been lost on adults, who in growing numbers use IM systems at the office. In this article from *Maclean's*, writer Chris Wood describes the mania over instant messaging.

STUFFED ANIMALS FILL THE BOOKSHELF BEHIND Mira Barnett's desk, threatening to overrun the trophies she won for public speaking. A blue cordless telephone matches her bedroom's colour scheme. But these days, the Vancouver Grade 8 student is more likely to gab with friends over her PC than on her phone. Using one of half a dozen instant messaging programs available free from the Internet, Barnett converses by exchanging short text messages with friends down the block or as far away as Mexico. Opening duplicate windows on her computer screen, Barnett shows how she keeps several "chats" going at once. Most are with schoolmates. But she also stays in touch with a Los Angeles friend and practises

■

From "A Mania for Messaging," by Chris Wood, *Maclean's*, November 13, 2000. Reprinted with permission.

her Hebrew with a 75-year-old woman in Israel whom she met on the Net. Among the advantages, the 12-year-old says, "you can make conversations with a whole bunch of people at once, and talk to your friends all over and not pay long distance."

The Hottest Social Advance Since the Mall

Mira's experience isn't likely to surprise anyone under the age of 20 with access to a computer—or their parents. Among Net-literate teenagers, instant messaging—which combines the immediacy of the phone with the brevity of e-mail text— has become the hottest social advance since the mall. Talky teenage girls seem particularly smitten by the technology, helping propel female users of the Internet to more than half of total users for the first time. But the young are not alone. As the growing popularity of instant messaging (IM) outstrips that of either regular e-mail or conventional Web-browsing, adults and businesses are waking up to its potential. Much of that is to the good, saving time and boosting productivity. But not all: experts worry that IM exposes already overloaded workers to yet another powerful distraction. "It is one of the major concerns of our clients," says John West, president of Priority Management Inc., a Vancouver company that trains executives in 16 countries. "They're leaving important projects undone and getting less important e-mail attended to."

Nonetheless, IM's rise has made the sector a rare hot spot of Web commerce, and driven the topic to centre stage in the debate over America Online's proposed $205-billion takeover of Time Warner Inc. [The merger was finalized on January 11, 2001.] AOL's two IM services—ICQ (for "I seek you") and AIM (AOL Instant Messenger)—account for an estimated 80 to 90 per cent of the world's 140 million or so registered instant-message users. Rivals, including giant Microsoft with its MSN Messenger program (No. 2 in popularity in Canada after ICQ, according to research firm Media Metrix Canada), [wanted] regulators to loosen AOL's hold on those customers before approving the mega-merger.

At its heart, IM gives anyone with an Internet connection access to the same type of real-time chat that users of large corporate, academic or government networks have long enjoyed. Unlike conventional Internet e-mail, which can sometimes take hours or even days to reach its destination, IM systems deliver the message just as the name suggests—instantly. A flashing on-screen icon or sound alerts recipients. Moreover, while e-mail is open to all, IM networks are closed: users can only message others who subscribe to the same service.

Buddy Lists

That is half the trick. The other half is something IM users know by the name "buddy lists," but engineers call "presence awareness." This is the software that makes it possible for people logging on to know who else among their list of friends is online at the same time. Alli Aziz, for instance, has about 20 names on her buddy list—all belonging to friends from her London, Ontario, elementary school. Like Mira Barnett, 12-year-old Aziz usually pursues more than one chat thread at a time, with different individuals or groups. "The most I've ever had going at once," she says, "was five."

Alli's mom understands the appeal. She doesn't use instant

Message-Speak

Instant messengers have spread and intensified the quick-typing, rarely capitalized vocabulary of online chat rooms. Translated samples:

sup? Whassup? (Similar to howzigoin)
nm Nothing much (or spelled out, nutin)
a/s/l? Age/sex/location? (Meaning, who r u?)
stats Answered by: brown hair, 115 lb. . . .
oic I get it
kewl Rhymes with, but does not describe, skool
rox It rox, they rawk
brb Be right back
wth What the, er, heck. Sometimes wtf
cu See you . . .
l8r . . . Later

Chris Wood, *Maclean's*, November 13, 2000.

messaging at home, but her employer's e-mail system operates much like an IM service, showing an alert whenever a new communication arrives. "I do find it's compulsive," Kathy Glasgow says. "I'm probably a little obsessed about checking it and getting back to people right away." But as director of records services at London's St. Joseph's Health Care Centre, Glasgow also keenly appreciates the swiftness with which a well-timed message exchange can resolve an issue. "The benefits outweigh the distraction," she concludes.

Millions agree. Forrester Research, which gathers Net statistics, estimates that [as of November 2000] more than a third of Web-connected North Americans use IM at least weekly. Within 18 months, an industry group expects the number of regular users to more than triple. That growth rate is one reason AOL's rivals are pushing so hard to loosen the Dulles, Virginia-based Internet giant's hold on IM. The bigger one is the future profits corporate strategists believe IM will unlock. Because users access IM services frequently, and often keep their windows open on-screen for long periods, those windows make appealing delivery vehicles for e-commerce advertising. IM is also being launched for cellphones and personal digital assistants like the Palm. Many analysts believe instant messaging is emerging as the "killer app" [application] of wireless.

For it to reach its fullest potential, however, existing barriers between different IM networks must fall, allowing open communication among users of all services—just as conventional e-mail does. . . . AOL [had] refused to open AIM and ICQ to such inter-operability, citing unspecified security concerns. Its rivals, including Microsoft, Yahoo! and AT&T, are working on a protocol to get the services working together. . . . [The U.S. Federal Communications Commission approved the AOL and Time Warner merger on the condition that AOL cooperate with its rivals.]

IM Will Also Include Voice

Other companies, meanwhile, are looking for their own share of messaging profits. Several have developed programs that let IM users communicate directly by voice using microphones and speakers built into their computers—in effect turning their PCs into telephones. Both MSN Messenger and AIM now offer free calls from computers directly to phone numbers across North America. [In October 2000] Eyeball.com of Vancouver launched a video-chat service that lets IM users equipped with PC video cameras see each other.

Down the road, believes Toronto market analyst Charley Whaley, "IM could become the glue that finally makes the Holy Grail of 'unified messaging' possible." Presence-awareness software will deliver incoming messages from any source to whatever digital device you happen to be using—PC, cellphone, pager or PDA [personal digital assistant]—translating text to voice (or vice versa) as necessary. Many older Canadians may feel information overload has reached a bewildering new level. Chances are Alli Aziz and Mira Barnett will feel right at home.

3

EXAMINING POP CULTURE

Transforming Popular Entertainment

Internet-Based Entertainment: A World of Possibilities

Gemma Tarlach

No one really knows how the Internet will affect the world of popular entertainment, but as Gemma Tarlach of the *Milwaukee Sentinel-Journal* reports, many people are making predictions. Many of these are extremist, with some observers saying the Internet will revolutionize entertainment and others worrying that it will harm popular culture. In the middle are industry insiders who believe that the Internet will not have little impact on the kinds of entertainment people enjoy. Instead, technology will allow people easier access to entertainment and give them more control over how and when they enjoy their favorite music, movies, and television shows.

BETTER. FASTER. CHEAPER. CUSTOMIZED. OPTImized. Revolutionized.

All of us are caught in the Charybdis of Internet-based entertainment—whether you own a computer or not, you can't avoid getting sucked into the whirlpool of hype about a cyberfuture—and the promises swirling around us are taking on mythic proportions.

More than two-thirds of Americans are already online, and [by 2005], most analysts believe an Internet connection of

■

some kind will be as common in the average American home as a telephone or TV set is now.

For the music industry, online distribution and marketing are already a reality; television and movies are catching up quickly, with e-books close behind. The Internet is even affecting the visual arts and theater.

Sorting Through the Hype

But just as forecasters can't agree on what shape our future household Internet connection will take—will the average setup include a high-speed cable modem or a DSL line, a desktop computer or a stereo/TV/VCR hybrid with online access?—no one is really sure how the convergence of entertainment and the Internet will change our pop culture landscape.

"Some people are saying, 'The Internet will create millions of isolated communities and we'll never interact with each other face-to-face,'" said Douglas Rushkoff, author of seven books on the Internet and pop culture, including "Cyberia."

"Other people say that three corporations will own everything and we'll all see the same thing, do the same things and become a monoculture," Rushkoff said. "But what we're really wrestling with is a problem that has been with human society since the beginning of civilization: How do you retain your individuality and yet function as a part of a larger system?"

The continuing search for balancing self and society has been obscured by hype for and against the Internet as a whole, and Internet-based entertainment in particular. Extremist predictions are dominating pop culture prognostication.

One school of thought believes we'll be able to personalize our entertainment options like never before, making our lives more interesting and fulfilling.

"If you love bowling, you'll be able to have the Bowling Channel, all day, every day, for example," said Jim Barry, spokesman for the Consumer Electronics Manufacturing Association.

The more pessimistic camp warns that such personalization in Internet-based entertainment will fragment not only pop culture, but eventually our society. We will lose first the shared experience, and then the experience of sharing.

"What are the problems of our society? Do our citizens have too few ways of entertaining themselves?" asked Clifford

Stoll, author of "High Tech Heretic" and a self-described Luddite. "Do we not watch enough TV? Do we spend too much time outdoors doing things, talking with our neighbors? Time we spend online is time we spend not doing something else."

As the Internet becomes less of a stranger in our daily entertainment consumption, however, a third, more moderate point of view is emerging: The Internet is just a new yet neutral means of distributing entertainment content; our culture will continue to support both mainstream and fringe forms of entertainment and expression.

Increased Access, Greater Control

"When the dust settles," predicted Scott Sander, CEO of Sightsound.com, "the future will look like today does—only a lot more convenient."

Within the next two to five years, most Internet observers believe that the average American's access to the online world of entertainment will increase exponentially. As high-speed Internet access—cable modems and DSL lines—become commonplace in the American home, we will be able to download video-quality (or better) movies and better-than-CD-quality music in minutes.

Along with faster downloading times and better sound and visuals, we are likely to have greater-than-ever control over our individual entertainment consumption.

Early forms of personalization technology are already on shelves. Devices called personal video recorders can scan available programming and record shows based on your preferences. You then watch the programs at your leisure, creating your own personal prime time.

Some observers worry that this customizability will not only isolate us physically, but, eventually, will cheapen our entertainment experiences.

"Instead of valuing an experience as rare, we'll say, so what, I've seen that on the Internet," said Stoll, who added that if we have the opportunity to go, say, virtual sky-diving from our living rooms, we'll be less likely to go out and do it for real.

Not everyone agrees, however.

"The assumption that people will replace the real with the virtual is baloney—it's sheer speculation," said Lutz Erbring, co-author of a recent, large-scale study by the Stanford Institute for the Quantitative Study of Society that examined the social effects of Internet usage. "There will be some things online that will be called 'the next best thing to being there'—but that's still the next best thing. It's not a substitute."

In the Stanford study, Erbring and his colleagues found that, in general, the time an individual spends online comes out of time spent watching TV rather than time spent interacting with people face-to-face or engaged in physical activity.

"I see real experiences as being valued more," said "Cyberia" author Rushkoff, who considers himself a moderate in the Internet entertainment debate. "Real life experiences have a granularity, a texture that we can't replicate.

"Look at music," Rushkoff added. "As we got better at digital recording, we started to gravitate toward more digital kinds of music. But you still have people throwing each other around in a mosh pit."

Changes in Distribution

As high-speed Internet access becomes commonplace in the next two to five years, expect the most significant changes in entertainment to be distribution rather than content.

"Everything will change about how you get your entertainment," said Sander of Sightsound.com, one of the first firms to sell downloadable movies and music. "But nothing will change about what that entertainment is. A couple thousand years ago, Aristotle wrote 'The Poetics,' which was your basic three acts, with everything resolved by the third act. That hasn't changed. It doesn't matter whether it's coming to you on a videotape, over TV or on the Internet."

Consider this: Throughout human history, our storytellers have repeated the same basic plot lines—love, lust, hero quests, betrayal and redemption. Generally speaking, what's changed over the centuries has been the delivery method of those tales. We've gone from fireside pantomimes in caves (perhaps the original interactive entertainment) to court-enthralling bards and dime novels to movies, television and now Net-delivered entertainment. In April, for example, Sander's Sightsound.com reached an agreement with major Hollywood player Miramax Films to provide encryption and processing of rental fees for downloadable Miramax flicks. Customers will download the movies and pay online (using a credit card) for a given rental period.

The movie files will expire after the prepaid rental period is up. The transaction will be entirely online, no plastic video cases or "please be kind, rewind" reminder involved—but the movies folks will be able to download will be the same ones available at the corner Blockbuster.

This ongoing distribution revolution will have an impact on our society—eventually, as more people opt for download-ing movies, the number of corner video and music stores will likely dwindle.

Just as vintage vinyl record stores live on, however, don't expect the total extinction of "brick and mortar" video stores.

Established " brands" such as Blockbuster are already beef-ing up their Internet presence, and will likely move to online operations as high-speed Internet access reaches more homes and makes downloading flicks feasible for the general public.

What about the mom-and-pop video and music stores?

"When automobiles hit the streets, what did the buggy manufacturers do?" posits Steve Devick, CEO of Platinum, one of the largest independent music labels and an early con-vert to Netertainment. "They found other jobs or they went out of business."

"A Slightly Altered New World"

Look for savvy entrepreneurs to turn empty storefronts into cybercafes and virtual reality arcades. Whether it's trading in the horse-drawn wagon for a pickup or moving your opera-tions from the street corner to cyberspace, humans have a knack for adapting.

Some Internet insiders say there was a brief window for new technology to have significant impact on our culture as a whole, including entertainment—but that such a time has passed.

"Back in the old days—about 1988 to 1994—people used their keyboards on the Internet. They communicated. They typed stories, expressed themselves. That had the potential for a major cultural shift," said Rushkoff. "But that opportunity was lost once people started browsing on the Internet, using their mouses to go from one site to the next rather than input their own content," he said. "We went from shareware and free expression based in university networks to companies developing proprietary software to make money off it."

As Netertainment evolves into a mature business, it's looking more and more like business as usual, with major brand names such as AOL dominating, but leaving room on the fringes for independents to provide alternative content.

"You'll watch 'Who Wants to be a Millionaire'—which people enjoy watching because it's a spectacle. It's like walking into a huge arena, and people like to feel they're part of something larger than themselves," said Rushkoff. "And, although not everybody would want to be part of, say, a medical discussion on kidney replacement, communities for those narrow areas of interest will also exist.

"Internet-based entertainment is not a good thing or a bad thing," Rushkoff concluded. "It's not an evolutionary jump forward or backward. It's just a slightly altered new world."

It's Time to Turn the Last Page

Steven Levy

Newsweek reporter Steven Levy predicts that as computers get even faster and the Internet becomes more widespread and easier to access, "e-books" will replace traditional books. These handheld devices will display text electronically rather than on paper and will be cheaper and easier to publish than conventional books. Because some authors may move from working directly with publishing houses to downloading their novels direct to a website, e-books will revolutionize the publishing industry. Because all of these new reading devices will be connected to the Internet, they will certainly change the way people read.

NO ONE IS CALLING THE 1900S THE CENTURY OF the Book. But you could make a case for it. For most of those years, the heavy hitters in our culture landed their big punches between the covers of bound boards: Joyce, Freud, Proust, Salinger, Orwell . . . even Bill Gates weighed in, twice. Sure, television eventually mesmerized the nation and the globe, but the number of books printed in the fading century surely dwarfed the production of all previous eras. And when e-commerce began, what did its flagship, Amazon.com, sell? Duh.

Still when Y3K pundits look back on our time, they'll remember it as the *Last* Century of the Book. Why? As a common item of communication, artistic expression and celebrity anecdote, the physical object consisting of bound dead trees in shiny wrapper is headed for the antique heap. Its replacement

■

will be a lightning-quick injection of digital bits into a hand-held device with an ultrasharp display. Culture vultures and bookworms might cringe at the prospect, but it's as inevitable as page two's following page one. Books are goners, at least as far as being the dominant form of reading.

Most of the pieces are already in place: fast chips, long-lasting batteries, capacious disk drives and the Internet. Only two things, really, hold us back from having reading devices that are just as felicitous as the dust-jacketed packages we know and love. One is high-speed wireless bandwidth, so that the devices can be quickly loaded. Fixing that is a no-brainer. No one doubts that such a big digital transmission system will show up early in the millennium.

The second is a screen whose output is as sumptuous as the current books', which engage not only our minds but our sense of touch. Oh, and having it cost so little that we won't hesitate to drag the thing to the beach or grab it on the way to the loo. In other words, cheap enough to lose.

What are the odds of that happening? Let's see. In the last 50 years, we've made computers thousands of times more powerful, while shrinking them from the size of a basketball court to something you can cradle in your palm. All the while dropping the price tag from millions of bucks to a few hundred. Does it really seem plausible that sometime next century we *can't* make a device that approximates the size and heft of a book or magazine, with a screen that's every bit as easy on the eyes as the Modern Library edition of *Sense and Sensibility*? Unless the world's computer scientists suddenly get struck stupid, we're going to get those devices, and they'll probably cost so little that we'll pay nothing for them—they'll be given away by content moguls so that we can buy more 21st-century news, pictures and literature. "The cards have been dealt," says Microsoft e-book czar Dick Brass. "The only difference is how fast people will play the hand."

Skeptics focus on the failings of the current generation of e-books. These are paperback-size readers with fairly clear type but backlit screens that don't compare with the things routinely shelved at the local Barnes & Noble. Still, I recently polished off a Stephen King novel in e-book form, an adventure tale involving a little girl lost in the woods. After a few screens' worth of King-speak, I was sufficiently sucked into the tale to pretty much forget about the medium, and I finished the novel in a few hours. I doubt that I would have gotten any more or less from it if I'd paged through the hardback.

Bottom line: you *can* use those things, even as unattractive and uncool as they are now. "And within five years," promises NuvoMedia CEO Martin Eberhard, "we'll have front-surface technology that doesn't require you to read behind glass." So it's easy to see how, when the reading experience gets better, e-books will overwhelmingly swamp the objections of book mavens like Sven Birkerts, a literary critic whose book *The Gutenberg Elegies* eloquently sheds tears over the coming purge. "The loss will be important, but it's elusive to specify," he says. "We'll miss the culture of the book, the envelope of associations."

An understandable complaint. But once we get past the question of *whether* the e-book will dominate, we can ponder a more interesting issue: What are the changes that will accompany the shift? The first big upheaval will come, of course, in

Books and Computers Will Coexist

The debate about the future of books is really about the relative performance of competing technologies. Books are designed by people, as are computers. There are plenty of examples of apparently irreconcilable disagreements over a new technology disappearing once the technology catches up to the specifications of what it's replacing. Many people used to religiously proclaim that they couldn't edit text on a computer screen; once the resolution of a screen began to approach that of the eye at a comfortable reading distance, the discussion began to go away. Now writing a text by hand is the exception rather than the rule. Such passionate debates get settled not by persuasion, but by technical progress making them increasingly irrelevant.

Along the way, the presumptions of a new technology must usually be tempered by the wisdom embodied in an old one. In the early days of the internal combustion en-the business of publishing. When publishers no longer have to focus on moving pulped forests to distributors, the business model will go bananas. "The turning point is going to come when one of the brand-name authors actually bolts and goes direct to readers," says one executive at a major publishing house, who even ventures a guess who that author might be: Stephen King. The master of horror is not only a perennial best seller, but a roll-the-dice kind of guy who's previously pulled headline-grabbing book-release stunts (like dribbling out *The Green Mile* in six easy pieces). So what's to stop him from selling *The Dead Again Zone* or some other 2004 thriller exclusively by $12 downloads in e-book format from StephenKing.com—and raking in a 100 percent royalty, after the relatively minimal expenses of formatting the book and maintaining the server? Such only-available-in-bit books would be the sort of killer app that spikes sales of e-readers. And after King does it, will Clancy, Grisham and Tom Wolfe be far behind?

When—not if—that happens, there will be widespread

gine it was interesting to race horses and cars. Now we have supersonic cars, but no one is arguing for the abolition of horses. Although horses are no longer the fastest means of transportation, no current car can recognize its owner with a glance, or choose a path through a narrow mountain pass, or be left in a meadow to refuel itself, or make a copy of itself when it begins to wear out. Cars still have a long way to go to catch up to horses. . . .

Choosing between books and computers makes as much sense as choosing between breathing and eating. Books do a magnificent job of conveying static information; computers let information change. We're just now learning how to use a lot of new technology to match the performance of the mature technology in books, transcending its inherent limits without sacrificing its best features. The bits and the atoms belong together. The story of the book is not coming to an end; it's really just beginning.

Neil Gershenfeld, *When Things Start to Think*, New York: Henry Holt, 1999.

panic on book row. After all, the profits of big-time book publishing these days involve shipping tons of would-be blockbusters and hoping that they don't come back unsold. Brand-name authors minimize the risk and reap the biggest profits. But if every brand-name author had the wherewithal to make it on his or her own by self-publishing e-books, the publishers might have to look elsewhere.

This could have a salutary effect on the business, and not just for authors and readers. For years we've been hearing about how publishers neglect the serious novels and nonfiction on what is known as the midlist. These are books launched with moderate advances on interesting subjects. Unlike tell-alls by murderers' girlfriends, memoirs of professional wrestlers and philosophical insights from stand-up comedians, these are the books that enable editors to look themselves in the mirror at night. Freed from fretting about the mechanics of distributing blockbusters, those editors might find time to carefully nurture books of quality—and be more aggressive in helping those books find their audiences. They'll have a great tool at hand: the Internet, perfect for identifying even the most obscure niches.

And if publishers don't concentrate their efforts on selling those midlist books more effectively? Then they could say goodbye to those authors, who will migrate to a new breed of electronic booksellers who will do just that.

In the long term, the e-book's most startling effect will involve what goes between the virtual covers. After all, the most notable feature of these new reading devices will be that all of them *will be connected to the Internet.* That simple fact will trigger profound changes.

First, watch for a change in the *way* we read. Physical books are discrete objects that open up to small worlds; connected e-books will offer *the* world. Only a few pokes on the touchscreen, and you're no longer in the middle of the novel you've been devouring—you're in the middle of some other book, or a critic's gloss on your reading material. Or maybe you're grooving to some streaming-audio tune. We may see the literary equivalent of channel surfing. "It will depreciate the author," laments Birkerts.

Finally, watch for the works themselves to change. Some kinds of books will instantly disappear. (Why would you want a static travel guide when you can instantly access all the up-to-date dope on any place in the world?) Familiar creative forms will slowly evolve to conform to the new medium. The novel, after all, fits neatly into the covers of physical books: long enough to be worth buying, but not too bulky to drag around. Without being confined by those physical limitations—and with the ability to include other kinds of digital media—creative minds will inevitably find new forms of expression. Will authors satisfy us with shorter stories? Lengthy tales that make *The Magic Mountain* look like a molehill? Soundtracks? Linguistic samplings that interweave new prose with previous classics or even random gatherings like ad copy or cartoons? Who knows? Just trust that every new medium finds its exploiters.

Meanwhile, true bibliophiles shouldn't get too broken up. The death of books won't necessarily mean the *disappearance* of books. Microsoft's Brass echoes the view of most observers when he says those of us raised on the pleasures of page turning and shelf browsing will ensure that all the world's volumes won't go up in one big *Fahrenheit 451* bonfire. "Books will persist because they're beautiful and useful," he says. "They're like horses after the automobile—not gone, but transformed into a recreational beast."

Video Games: The New Art Form of the Digital Age

Henry Jenkins

In the article below literature professor Henry Jenkins argues forcefully that video games are a new and emerging art form, not "cultural pollution," as some claim. The director of the Program in Comparative Media Studies at the Massachusetts Institute of Technology (MIT), Jenkins compares video games to silent pictures. Like videos, movies were reviled and dismissed in the 1920s, in part because they were too violent. By commenting on the content and technique of early films, serious film critics helped to mold movies into a respected art form. Jenkins hopes serious critics will play the same roll for video games. Like any new art form, he concludes, video games are controversial; they also are still evolving and maturing and most certainly will have a significant impact on culture.

■

LAST YEAR, AMERICANS BOUGHT OVER 215 MILlion computer and video games. That's more than two games per household. The video game industry made almost as much money from gross domestic income as Hollywood.

So are video games a massive drain on our income, time and energy? A new form of "cultural pollution," as one U.S. senator described them? The "nightmare before Christmas," in the words of another? Are games teaching our children to kill, as countless op-ed pieces have warned?

■

From "Art Form for the Digital Age," by Henry Jenkins, *Technology Review*, September/October 2000. Reprinted by permission of *Technology Review* via the Copyright Clearance Center.

Video Games Are Art

No. Computer games are art—a popular art, an emerging art, a largely unrecognized art, but art nevertheless.

[Since the 1970s,] games have progressed from the primitive two-paddles-and-a-ball Pong to the sophistication of Final Fantasy, a participatory story with cinema-quality graphics that unfolds over nearly 100 hours of play. The computer game has been a killer app [application] for the home PC, increasing consumer demand for vivid graphics, rapid processing, greater memory and better sound. The release this fall [2000] of the Sony Playstation 2, coupled with the announcement of next-generation consoles by Nintendo and Microsoft, signals a dramatic increase in the resources available to game designers.

Games increasingly influence contemporary cinema, helping to define the frenetic pace and model the multi-directional plotting of *Run Lola Run*, providing the role-playing metaphor for *Being John Malkovich* and encouraging a fascination with the slippery line between reality and digital illusion in *The Matrix*. At high schools and colleges across the country, students discuss games with the same passions with which earlier generations debated the merits of the New American Cinema. Media studies programs report a growing number of their students want to be game designers rather than filmmakers.

Time to Take Games Seriously

The time has come to take games seriously as an important new popular art shaping the aesthetic sensibility of the 21st century. I will admit that discussing the art of video games conjures up comic images: tuxedo-clad and jewel-bedecked patrons admiring the latest Streetfighter, middle-aged academics pontificating on the impact of Cubism on Tetris, bleeps and zaps disrupting our silent contemplation at the Guggenheim. Such images tell us more about our contemporary notion of art—as arid and stuffy, as the property of an educated and economic elite, as cut off from everyday experience—than they tell us about games.

New York's Whitney Museum found itself at the center of controversy about digital art when it recently included Web artists in its prestigious biannual show. Critics didn't believe the computer could adequately express the human spirit. But they're misguided. The computer is simply a tool, one that offers artists new resources and opportunities for reaching the public; it is human creativity that makes art. Still, one can only imagine how the critics would have responded to the idea that something as playful, unpretentious and widely popular as a computer game might be considered art.

Other Art Forms Were Also Once Rejected

In 1925, leading literary and arts critic Gilbert Seldes took a radical approach to the aesthetics of popular culture in a treatise titled *The Seven Lively Arts*. Adopting what was then a controversial position, Seldes argued that America's primary contributions to artistic expression had come through emerging forms of popular culture such as jazz, the Broadway musical, the Hollywood cinema and the comic strip. While these arts have gained cultural respectability over the past 75 years, each was disreputable when Seldes staked out his position.

Readers then were skeptical of Seldes' claims about cinema in particular for many of the same reasons that contemporary critics dismiss games—they were suspicious of cinema's commercial motivations and technological origins, concerned about Hollywood's appeals to violence and eroticism, and insistent that cinema had not yet produced works of lasting value. Seldes, on the other hand, argued that cinema's popularity demanded that we reassess its aesthetic qualities.

Cinema and other popular arts were to be celebrated, Seldes said, because they were so deeply imbedded in everyday life, because they were democratic arts embraced by average citizens. Through streamlined styling and syncopated rhythms, they captured the vitality of contemporary urban experience. They took the very machinery of the industrial age, which many felt dehumanizing, and found within it the resources for expressing individual visions, for reasserting basic human needs, desires and fantasies. And these new forms were still open to experimentation and discovery. They were, in Seldes' words, "lively arts."

Art for the Digital Age

Games represent a new lively art, one as appropriate for the digital age as those earlier media were for the machine age.

They open up new aesthetic experiences and transform the computer screen into a realm of experimentation and innovation that is broadly accessible. And games have been embraced by a public that has otherwise been unimpressed by much of what passes for digital art. Much as the salon arts of the 1920s seemed sterile alongside the vitality and inventiveness of popular culture, contemporary efforts to create interactive narrative through modernist hypertext or avant-garde installation art seem lifeless and pretentious alongside the creativity that game designers bring to their craft.

Much of what Seldes told us about the silent cinema seems remarkably apt for thinking about games. Silent cinema, he argued, was an art of expressive movement. He valued the speed and dynamism of [director] D.W. Griffith's last-minute races to the rescue, the physical grace of Chaplin's pratfalls and the ingenuity of [comic actor] Buster Keaton's engineering feats. Games also depend upon an art of expressive movement, with characters defined through their distinctive ways of propelling themselves through space, and successful products structured around a succession of spectacular stunts and predicaments. Will future generations look back on [the heroine of the video game Tomb Raider] Lara Croft doing battle with a pack of snarling wolves as the 21st-century equivalent of [silent screen actress] Lillian Gish making her way across the ice floes in *Way Down East*? The art of silent cinema was also an art of atmospheric design. To watch a silent masterpiece like [director] Fritz Lang's *Metropolis* is to be drawn into a world where meaning is carried by the placement of shadows, the movement of machinery and the organization of space. If anything, game designers have pushed beyond cinema in terms of developing expressive and fantastic environments that convey a powerful sense of mood, provoke our curiosity and amusement, and motivate us to explore.

Seldes wrote at a moment when cinema was maturing as an expressive medium and filmmakers were striving to enhance the emotional experience of going to the movies—making a move from mere spectacle towards character and consequence. It remains to be seen whether games can make a similar transition. Contemporary games can pump us full of adrenaline, they can make us laugh, but they have not yet provoked us to tears. And many have argued that, since games don't have characters of human complexity or stories that stress the consequences of our actions, they cannot achieve the status of true art. Here, we must be careful not to confuse the current transitional state of an emerging medium with its full potential. As I visit game companies, I see some of the industry's best minds struggling with this question and see strong evidence that the games released over the next few years will bring us closer and closer to the quality of characterization we have come to expect from other forms of popular narrative.

Can We Care About Video Characters?

In the March 6 [2000] issue of *Newsweek*, senior editor Jack Kroll argued that audiences will probably never be able to care as deeply about pixels on the computer screen as they care about characters in films: "Moviemakers don't have to simulate human beings; they are right there, to be recorded and orchestrated. . . . The top-heavy titillation of Tomb Raider's Lara Croft falls flat next to the face of Sharon Stone. . . . Any player who's moved to tumescence by digibimbo Lara is in big trouble." Yet countless viewers cry when Bambi's mother dies, and World War II veterans can tell you they felt real lust for *Esquire*'s Vargas [sketched pin-up] girls. We have learned to care as much about creatures of pigment as we care about images of real people. Why should pixels be different?

In the end, games may not take the same path as cinema. Game designers will almost certainly develop their own aesthetic principles as they confront the challenge of balancing our competing desires for storytelling and interactivity. It remains to be seen whether games can provide players the freedom they want and still provide an emotionally satisfying and thematically meaningful shape to the experience. Some of the best games—Tetris comes to mind—have nothing to do with storytelling. For all we know, the future art of games may look more like architecture or dance than cinema.

Video Standards Are Still Evolving

Such questions warrant close and passionate engagement not only within the game industry or academia, but also by the press and around the dinner table. Even Kroll's grumpy dismissal of games has sparked heated discussion and forced designers to refine their own grasp of the medium's distinctive features. Imagine what a more robust form of criticism could contribute. We need critics who know games the way Pauline Kael knew movies and who write about them with an equal degree of wit and wisdom.

When *The Seven Lively Arts* was published, silent cinema was still an experimental form, each work stretching the medium in new directions. Early film critics played vital functions in documenting innovations and speculating about their potential. Computer games are in a similar phase. We have not had time to codify what experienced game designers know, and we have certainly not yet established a canon of great works that might serve as exemplars. There have been real creative accomplishments in games, but we haven't really sorted out what they are and why they matter.

But games *do* matter, because they spark the imaginations of our children, taking them on epic quests to strange new worlds. Games matter because our children no longer have access to real-world play spaces at a time when we've paved over the vacant lots to make room for more condos and the streets make parents nervous. If children are going to have opportunities for exploratory play, play that encourages cognitive development and fosters problem-solving skills, they will do so in the virtual environments of games. Multi-player games create opportunities for leadership, competition, teamwork and collaboration—for nerdy kids, not just for high-school football players. Games matter because they form the digital equivalent of the Head Start program, getting kids excited about what computers can do.

Realizing Video Games' Potential

The problem with most contemporary games isn't that they are violent but that they are banal, formulaic and predictable. Thoughtful criticism can marshal support for innovation and experimentation in the industry, much as good film criticism helps focus attention on neglected independent films. Thoughtful criticism could even contribute to our debates about game violence. So far, the censors and culture warriors have gotten more or less a free ride because we almost take for granted that games are culturally worthless. We should instead look at games as an emerging art form—one that does not simply simulate violence but increasingly offers new ways to understand violence—and talk about how to strike a balance between this form of expression and social responsibility. Moreover, game criticism may provide a means of holding the game industry more accountable for its choices. In the wake of the Columbine shootings, game designers are struggling with their ethical responsibilities as never before, searching for ways of appealing to empowerment fantasies that don't require exploding heads and gushing organs. A serious public discussion of this medium might constructively influence these debates, helping identify and evaluate alternatives as they emerge.

As the art of games matures, progress will be driven by the most creative and forward-thinking minds in the industry, those who know that games can be more than they have been, those who recognize the potential of reaching a broader public, of having a greater cultural impact, of generating more diverse and ethically responsible content and of creating richer and more emotionally engaging stories. But without the support of an informed public and the perspective of thoughtful critics, game developers may never realize that potential.

The Movies' Film-Less Future

Lewis Beale

Digitized special effects are becoming increasingly common in Hollywood feature films. Using computer technology, filmmakers have created digitized spaceships, monsters, and tornadoes that look convincingly lifelike on screen.

Director George Lucas's *Star Wars: Episode I— The Phantom Menace*, released in 1999, incorporated more digitized special effects than any film had before. Below, New York *Daily News* writer Lewis Beale reports on *Star Wars: Episode II*, due out in 2002. The film is planned as the first major Hollywood feature to be made entirely with computer technology. The film will not be entirely computer-generated, since it will use real actors—but it will be shot entirely on digital video rather than on traditional film. As Beale reports, the advent of digital cinematography has many filmmakers excited, but it will be several years before digital video is as widely used as film.

GEORGE LUCAS THINKS FILM IS DEAD.

And traditional movie projectors.

And maybe just about every way movies will go from a Hollywood set to the local Bijou.

Lucas has totally embraced the new concept of digital production, distribution and projection. His "Star Wars: Episode II"—due out next year—is the first major Hollywood live-action movie made entirely by using computerized digital

■

technology. The likely blockbuster doesn't contain a single frame of film.

Sound, color, widescreen—there have been only three major technological advances since the advent of movies in the late 19th century. Now, digital science promises to open up a whole new way of shooting and showing films.

The Promise of Digital Cinematography

Ideally, digital technology—which translates what would normally be a picture on film into computer language—allows film makers to shoot in a format that's cheaper than film but can simulate the rich look of celluloid.

The finished product then can be downloaded onto a DVD disk and sent via satellite or cable to your neighborhood theater. And because the movie has been converted to digital language,

Hollywood Adapts Slowly to the Internet

The Internet and technology have been heavily promoted by Hollywood newcomers, who now wield a great deal of influence in the movie business. In this excerpt from his article on the Internet's challenge to Hollywood, Red Herring *writer Robert La Franco maintains that in spite of the current chaos, Hollywood's major studios will survive and even adapt.*

When television sets arrived in Hollywood in the 1940s, the story goes, the legendary Jack Warner had them thrown off the studio's lot. He was convinced—wrongly, as it turned out—that the new device would kill his thriving movie business. Flash forward half a century, and you find that Hollywood's establishment hasn't changed that much. . . .

The revolution will be much more complete than ever imagined by Jack Warner. Internet audiences will be very different from the ones the entertainment industry has served through every other medium it has known. Other media have depended on linear content: spoon-feed a pas-

when it is projected onscreen there are none of film's inevitable drawbacks: no color fading, scratches, wobbles or flutters. Every showing of the movie will be as clear and crisp as the first.

"What's so exciting about digital cinematography is that we are finally getting closer to the ultimate goal of being able to distribute and exhibit the movie digitally," says "Star Wars" producer Rick McCallum.

Yet despite the hype about digital film making over the last few years, its time has not quite come.

"Digital is not all the way there yet," says Mark Gill of Miramax, a company that has been in the forefront of digital experimentation. "The exhibition part is proven, but the production part has not been proven yet in a commercial, highly visible way."

sive viewer a story from start to finish. The Internet poses new problems. Yes, families will still gather around televisions, and teenagers will go to multiplexes, but soon everyone will listen, watch, and use entertainment on a variety of different devices—from PCs and cell phones to shopping mall kiosks. And entertainment may look very different in the era of interactive services. . . .

There are short film sites IFilm and AtomFilms, animation sites Shockwave.com and Icebox, edgy short program sites WireBreak and Pseudo. On the high-pedigree end: Dream Works, Imagine Entertainment, and Paul Allen are building Pop.com, a short-program Web site, while Brad Grey and IdeaLab are creating Z, a channel for comedy, music, and other diversions. . . .

Is entertainment as we know it soon to be forgotten? Are the studios doomed? Will agents finally be forced into humility? Hardly. The old world of media will do fine. The studios' massive libraries will always have residual value. And as the edgy newcomers pave the way, the studios will learn—slowly—how to adapt to the new style.

Robert La Franco, "Faces of a New Hollywood?" *Red Herring*, April 2000.

That may happen when "Star Wars: Episode II" hits the multiplex in spring 2002. Lucas made it using a new camera developed by Sony, Lucasfilm and Panavision.

But digital video has already become a common tool for low-budget and independent film makers, used in such productions as "Chuck and Buck" and "Dancer in the Dark," and for such major studio animated films as "Dinosaur" and "A Bug's Life."

Because the format is highly light-sensitive, film makers can shoot without extensive lighting systems, which means faster setups, smaller crews and lower costs. Yet the downside can be a big one, especially for those who don't have access to the new Lucasfilm camera—and that's just about everyone.

"The picture quality is inferior," says Derek Walker, first assistant cameraman on "Nine Scenes About Love," an indie film that recently finished shooting in New York. "How [inferior]? People have to make that judgment for themselves."

Part of the problem is that videotape has to be converted to film so it can be exhibited in theaters. And when that happens, it tends to look like video. Not that this is a problem for some people. "Digital feels intimate," says "Nine Scenes About Love" co-producer Jason Kliot. "You're used to watching newsreel footage and home video, so even when it's transferred to film, there's an immediacy."

Saving Millions

But film prints can cost as much as $2,500 each, which can add as much as $7.5 million to a film's budget. Some experts estimate that Hollywood studios could save hundreds of millions of dollars in print costs if they switched to digital—which is why digital projection seems to be the key to the whole computerized film making revolution.

Here, too, cost is a big issue. Digital projection systems cost $100,000 each, nearly 10 times more than a 35mm projector. Only about 30 theaters in the world are equipped with digital projection equipment; two of those screens are at the AMC Empire 25 on W. 42nd St., which has shown digital versions of such shot-on-film features as "The Perfect Storm," "Bounce" and "Titan A.E."

The basic difference between digital and film projection is

that in the digital format, the movie comes on a DVD, which is downloaded into a projector that's essentially a computer. An operator programs the showtimes, and only comes into the booth to make sure things are running smoothly.

"The improvement in image quality is an up for us," AMC's Rick King says of the projectors. "We believe, and the customers have told us, that the quality of the digital presentation is now superior to film." But because of the high costs, neither AMC nor any other major chain is rushing to install digital equipment. Down the line, however, it appears film studios and theater owners will share conversion costs. That could be three to five years from now. In the meantime, the biggest question in the industry is not whether digital is coming—it is—but whether it will replace film.

"No," says Bob Harvey of Panavision. "This is a format, the same way film is a format. Depending on the script, or the way a director wants to tell a story, they could use [digital], or they could use film."

Adds Steven Douglas Smith, a cinematographer who has shot digital features: "This new format is not film. It is still digital. The look is unique. You can cheat and make it look as film-like as possible, but it's not film."

The MP3 Revolution: Shaking Up the Music Industry

Charles C. Mann

Personal music collections have traditionally con-
sisted of records, tapes, and CDs. But in the 1990s, it
became possible to download music directly to a PC
without paying a dime. Two technical advancements
made these high-caliber downloads practicable. First
MP3, a method for shrinking music data files, made
it possible to store once unwieldy music files on a
personal computer. Then Napster—a software developed by teenager Shawn Fanning—enabled people to
browse and then download each other's MP3 music
files. In short order the Recording Industry Association of America sued to stop this practice. The courts
will be left to decide how the intellectual property
rights of musicians can be protected in a networked
world and how companies like Napster can legally
put music on the Web. In this article for *The Atlantic
Monthly*, contributing editor Charles C. Mann defines
"MP3," describes how it works, and introduces
MP3.com, an alternative music company. He also explains how this technology and companies like
MP3.com might affect the music industry and why
musicians and recording companies are so worried.

■

ONE OF THE ODDEST THINGS ABOUT THE INTERnet is that despite its purportedly revolutionary nature, it has yet to produce anything revolutionary. Shopping without actually visiting a store? Catalogues have let people do the same thing for decades. Instant communication over global distances? Available since the invention of the telegraph. Electronic mail? A century ago, most urban areas had so many daily postal deliveries that people could exchange several messages a day. Instant, uncontrollable diffusion of information? Despite Victor Hugo's efforts in 1862 to control the publication of *Les Misérables*, which included sequestering the galleys, pirate publishers produced eleven bootleg editions of his mammoth novel in Belgium alone within a week of its appearance. The technological tools are faster and more efficient today than they were before, but they're not different in kind.

A Method to Shrink Digital Sound Files

Technically speaking, MP3 is just a method for shrinking digital sound files, especially files of music, to a more manageable size. More than that, though, MP3 is a marvelously clear example of how an apparently small technological change can have unexpected and explosive impacts on society. Indeed, MP3 might become the first innovation on the Net that actually deserves the appellation "revolutionary."

The term "MP3" is—horrible to contemplate—an abbreviation of an abbreviation. It stands for "MPEG-1 Layer 3," a technical standard created by the Moving Picture Experts Group, an ad hoc organization based in Italy and supervised jointly by the International Organization for Standardization and the International Electrotechnical Commission. Coordinated by Leonardo Chiariglione, an engineer at the Italian equivalent of the old Bell Labs, MPEG has been creating standards for digital video and audio since 1988. The standards involve transmitting, storing, and reproducing pictures and sounds, and, perhaps most important, shrinking them. Converted into digital form, images and noises become huge, multimegabyte agglomerations of zeroes and ones that simply overwhelm many networks. Asking a personal computer to project a movie on a monitor or play a symphony on its speakers is like asking it to push the ocean through a straw.

In the past few decades, computer scientists have figured out methods to compress parts of these agglomerations while maintaining their essential character, in somewhat the way that I can write "Atlntc Unbnd" to mean "Atlantic Unbound." In the late 1980s, one of these shrinkage schemes was jointly developed by the University of Erlangen, in Germany, and the Institut Integrierte Schaltungen (Institute for Integrated Circuits), a nearby think tank. It decreased the size of music files by a factor of twelve or more, which today permits a typical four-minute rock song to be downloaded into a typically equipped personal computer in something like five minutes. When MPEG embraced this method, one of three different compression methods the group endorsed, it became known as the "third layer" of the first MPEG standard: MPEG-1 Layer 3.

Think Tank Distributes the MP3 "Shareware"

In 1995, the Institut began distributing "shareware" for making MP3 files—that is, programs that anyone could download for free, try out, and pay for later. The technology, says Chiariglione, was originally targeted at a type of interactive compact disc—CD-I, marketed by Philips—that no longer exists. It was also intended for digital radio, which doesn't exist, either. Nobody at MPEG realized how quickly the Net would become ubiquitous, Chiariglione says. Or how quickly personal computers would become cheap and powerful enough to use MP3. As a result, the inventors of this technology were as surprised as everyone else by what MP3 software would be used for, and by who would use it. Or, to put it more exactly: they didn't foresee Blex.

Blex is the online name of Michael Kramer. According to his autobiographical Web page, Blex is a six-foot, 145-lb., eighteen-year-old McDonald's grill person of the month and fan of power-symphonic-German-progressive-death-metal music. He enters the story in the spring of 1997, on the occasion of his senior prom, which he did not attend. "There was nothing to do," his autobiography explains, "seeing that all the people I know were at the prom, and I was at home." Noodling around the Web in what would seem to have been his ample spare time, Blex had previously come across several sites on the Internet where people had placed MP3 files: songs that they had illicitly copied from audio CDs, compressed with MP3 software, and put on the Web for people to download freely. Bored on prom night, Blex decided to list these places on his personal Web page.

Word got around. People sent him more URLs. He put them up, attracting more visitors, who passed on more URLs. Eventually Blex had pointers to thousands of songs, more than ten thousand daily visitors to his Web page, the belief that he had "made a difference in the world"—and, last year [1998], the angry attention of Jim Griffin, the director of technology for Geffen Records.

Music Companies Take Notice

Geffen wasn't the only company blindsided by Blex and his cohorts. None of the big music studios had imagined that thousands of high school and college students with Pentium PCs would be willing to spend hours downloading music and playing it on their computers. But they were. Only in 1997—as people on five continents eagerly sought MP3 information from the Blexes of the world—did the studios launch a campaign against illicitly copied music on the Internet. Their vehicle for the battle was the Recording Industry Association of America, a trade group that represents about 350 record labels. RIAA issued bulletins, sent nasty letters, filed a few lawsuits, and complained in the media. It successfully lobbied Capitol Hill to pass the strict guidelines in the Digital Millennium Copyright Act. It persuaded Johnny Cash to testify in Congress about finding bootleg copies of his classic rendition of "Ring of Fire" on an MP3 site in Slovenia. And last December the association announced its plan to create a security standard that somehow would let studios control the use of their copyrighted material on the Internet. RIAA says its standard should be ready for Christmas 1999.

Maybe it will work, and piracy will be cut back. But it may not matter. For all the attention lavished on pirated MP3 music, the real threat faced by the studios may be *legal* MP3 music, according to Hal Varian, the dean of the School of Information Management Systems at the University of California at Berkeley, and a co-author, with his colleague Carl Shapiro, of *Information Rules.*

Varian says, in effect: Consider the economics of music. Right now the music business is dominated by a handful of large studios with a history of antipathy to electronic technology. Fearing unauthorized reproduction, these companies fought the advent of cassette recorders, managed almost to stop the introduction of digital audio tapes, and are trying to fight off the impact of MP3. In economic terms, the record labels were wrong about cassettes, which have become an industry profit center, and might have been wrong for the same reasons about digital audio tape. But they could be right to fear MP3, which could replace rather than enhance their traditional business. "They have this terrible problem with their legacy," Varian says. "They still have to be in bed with Tower Records to sell their CDs. Any move they make to go on the Net will be instantly punished by their current distributors." This bind, in Varian's view, creates room for what economists call new entrants to the market. In less abstract terms, it opens the gate for MP3.com.

MP3.com

Located on the northern edge of San Diego, MP3.com is an alternative version of the music business, based entirely on MP3, personal computers, and the Internet. MP3.com provides music over the Internet. Not one note belongs to the members of the RIAA. Instead, MP3.com allows musicians who can't or won't get contracts with record labels to upload their own music onto the company's computers for free. In return the musicians must provide one song that the public can download gratis. If listeners like that song, they can click a button and order a CD by the artist. The CDs are stamped out on demand, uploaded as files, and mailed directly to customers' homes. MP3.com gives its artists half the price of the CD. No overhead, no overstocking, no complicated royalty arrangements—and, perhaps most important, no A&R.

A&R is music-industry lingo for "artists and repertoire." It refers to that part of the business involved with selecting and marketing musicians. Because a large number of different composers and performers cannot be promoted simultaneously by a single organization, the studios' A&R departments perforce function as gatekeepers, choosing a small number of musicians on whom to lavish attention and spurning the rest. MP3.com, by contrast, doesn't market its bands, and hence doesn't discriminate among them. The most inept crew—the group I played drums for in college, for example—can upload its music and have it presented by MP3.com in exactly the same way that the Web site presents expert professional musicians. "The difference is that the market for your group will be smaller than the market for the group with talent," says Michael Robertson, the founder of MP3.com. "You might be able to convince a few friends and relatives to buy your CD from us, but the other group, if it's any good, has a chance to get some word of mouth going."

Unknown Musicians Get a Chance

Word of mouth? Isn't this treading close to one of the major intellectual debates around the Web? As readers of last fall's [1998] *Atlantic Unbound* roundtable discussion on copyright may recall, John Perry Barlow—cattle rancher, Grateful Dead lyricist, civil-liberties activist, and Internet theoretician—argued that cyberspace, "like any ecosystem, [is] developing a remarkable ability to collectively distinguish nutrients from toxins." On the Net, Barlow posited, gatekeepers like music studios and book publishers are not needed to select and present the best works, because "millions of people are conducting this great edit." Much or most of what appears online is trivial, but the best is always sorted out in an invisible sifting performed by countless minds. "Worthy material that might not pass through one narrow cultural filter," Barlow wrote, "may well be discovered and massively reproduced by another" to the benefit of all. In a way unlike any other entity on the Net, MP3.com is hoping to harness that "great edit" to make money for itself and for thousands of musicians.

The studios, for their part, scoff at the notion. "What are they going to do?" asks Jeffrey Neuberger, an attorney who represents several major labels. "Present you with an undifferentiated mass of music, most of which is garbage, and let you randomly browse through it, on the theory that maybe you might find something you like?" In Neuberger's view, the need for A&R is almost too obvious to be worth discussing.

I confess to having some sympathy for this view. But a recent visit to MP3.com headquarters gave me pause. Begun with next to no publicity—"hardly even a business plan," Robertson says—it is now adding 140 bands a day, and doubling its load of music every two months. The company's workforce has quintupled since the beginning of the year [1999]. Its Web pages receive more than two million page views a day, and the number keeps rising. The offices have expanded so rapidly that when I commented to Robertson about the unusual, polygonal sconces in the hallway he stared at them in surprise and then confessed he had been so busy that he had hardly looked around the new offices.

Music Culture Likely Will Change

At the least, MP3.com is an empirical experiment that will test both Barlow's rosy predictions and the skepticism of people like me. If the experiment succeeds, it will create hundreds or thousands of word-of-mouth musical communities. . . .

If this new method of distributing music becomes important, our musical culture will fragment even more than it already has. There may still be a few hugely popular artists—the Michael Jacksons and Luciano Pavarottis of tomorrow—but the rest will form hundreds of little cyberspace principalities of song, each with its separate base of support. To avoid being lost in the ether online, musicians will have to cultivate their public closely. Indeed, MP3.com is setting up a service that will allow bands to e-mail everyone who has bought their CDs. Rock stars today live like [eccentric multi-millionaire] Howard Hughes, providing their audience when not onstage with only fleeting glimpses of themselves at photo-ops for E! and *Spin*. No more aloofness in the future; instead of hiding from fans, the Jimmy Pages and The Edges of the future will be down at the mall, letting toddlers plunk on their Gibsons and Les Pauls.

EXAMINING *POP* CULTURE

New Problems for the Information Age

Falling Through the Net: The Digital Divide

National Telecommunications and Information Administration (NTIA)

In its third report in the *Falling Through the Net* series, the National Telecommunications and Information Administration (NTIA) reports that a serious gap exists between this country's "haves" and the "have nots" when it comes to access to computers and the Internet. The report's introduction notes that this digital divide is "now one of America's leading economic and civil rights issues." Minorities, people with low incomes, the less educated, children in single-parent households, and those living in rural areas or the inner city most often lack access to information technologies. Using 1998 U.S. Census Bureau data, the NTIA prepared a detailed report of more than one hundred pages. The portions excerpted below provide an overview of the problem and suggest ways in which government at all levels can help improve public access to the Internet.

INFORMATION TOOLS, SUCH AS THE PERSONAL computer and the Internet, are increasingly critical to economic success and personal advancement. *Falling Through the Net: Defining the Digital Divide* finds that more Americans than ever have access to telephones, computers, and the Internet. At the same time, however, the National Telecommunications

■

Excerpted from the Executive Summary of the report *Falling Through the Net: Defining the Digital Divide*, by the National Telecommunications and Information Administration (Washington, DC: U.S. Dept. of Commerce, 1999).

and Information Administration (NTIA) has found that there is still a significant "digital divide" separating American information "haves" and "have nots." Indeed, in many instances, the digital divide has *widened* in the last year [1998].

Americans Are More Connected than Ever

This report, NTIA's third in the *Falling Through the Net* series, relies on December 1998 U.S. Department of Commerce Census Bureau data to provide an updated snapshot of the digital divide. The good news is that Americans are more connected than ever before. Access to computers and the Internet has soared for people in all demographic groups and geographic locations. At the end of 1998, over 40 percent of American households owned computers, and one-quarter of all households had Internet access. Additionally, those who were less likely to have telephones (chiefly, young and minority households in rural areas) are now more likely to have phones at home.

Accompanying this good news, however, is the persistence of the digital divide between the information rich (such as Whites, Asians/Pacific Islanders, those with higher incomes, those more educated, and dual-parent households) and the information poor (such as those who are younger, those with lower incomes and education levels, certain minorities, and those in rural areas or central cities). The 1998 data reveal significant disparities, including the following:

- Urban households with incomes of $75,000 and higher are more than *twenty times* more likely to have access to the Internet than rural households at the lowest income levels, and more than *nine times* as likely to have a computer at home.
- Whites are more likely to have access to the Internet from home than Blacks or Hispanics have from *any* location.
- Black and Hispanic households are approximately *one-third* as likely to have home Internet access as households of Asian/Pacific Islander descent, and roughly *two-fifths* as likely as White households.
- Regardless of income level, Americans living in rural areas are lagging behind in Internet access. Indeed, at the lowest income levels, those in urban areas are more than

twice as likely to have Internet access than those earning the same income in rural areas.

For many groups, the digital divide has *widened* as the information "haves" outpace the "have nots" in gaining access to electronic resources. The following gaps with regard to home Internet access are representative:

- The gaps between White and Hispanic households, and between White and Black households, are now approximately five percentage points larger than they were in 1997.
- The digital divides based on education and income level have also increased in the last year alone. Between 1997 and 1998, the divide between those at the highest and lowest education levels increased 25 percent, and the divide between those at the highest and lowest income levels grew 29 percent.

Nevertheless, the news is not all bleak. For Americans with incomes of $75,000 and higher, the divide between Whites and Blacks has actually narrowed considerably in the last year. This finding suggests that the most affluent American families, irrespective of race, are connecting to the Net. If prices of computers and the Internet decline further, the divide between the information "haves" and "have nots" may continue to narrow.

Until every home can afford access to information resources, however, we will need public policies and private initiatives to expand affordable access to those resources. . . .

As we enter the Information Age, access to computers and the Internet is becoming increasingly vital. It is in everyone's interest to ensure that no American is left behind.

Challenges Ahead

Traditionally, our notion of being connected to the nation's communications networks has meant having a telephone. Today, Americans' increased use of computers and the Internet has changed that notion. To be connected today increasingly means to have access to telephones, computers, *and* the Internet. While these items may not be necessary for survival, arguably in today's emerging digital economy they are necessary for success. As the Department of Commerce has found in its *Emerging*

Digital Economy reports, the dramatic growth of electronic commerce and the development of information technology (IT) industries are changing the way Americans work, communicate, purchase goods, and obtain information. Jobs in the new economy now increasingly require technical skills and familiarity with new technologies. Additionally, obtaining services and information increasingly requires access to the Internet.

Policymakers have achieved high levels of telephone connectivity through the implementation of two key initiatives. Pro-competition policies at the state and national levels have resulted in lower prices for consumers of telephone services. Universal service policies have helped assure that most Americans can enjoy affordable access today. Assistance for low-

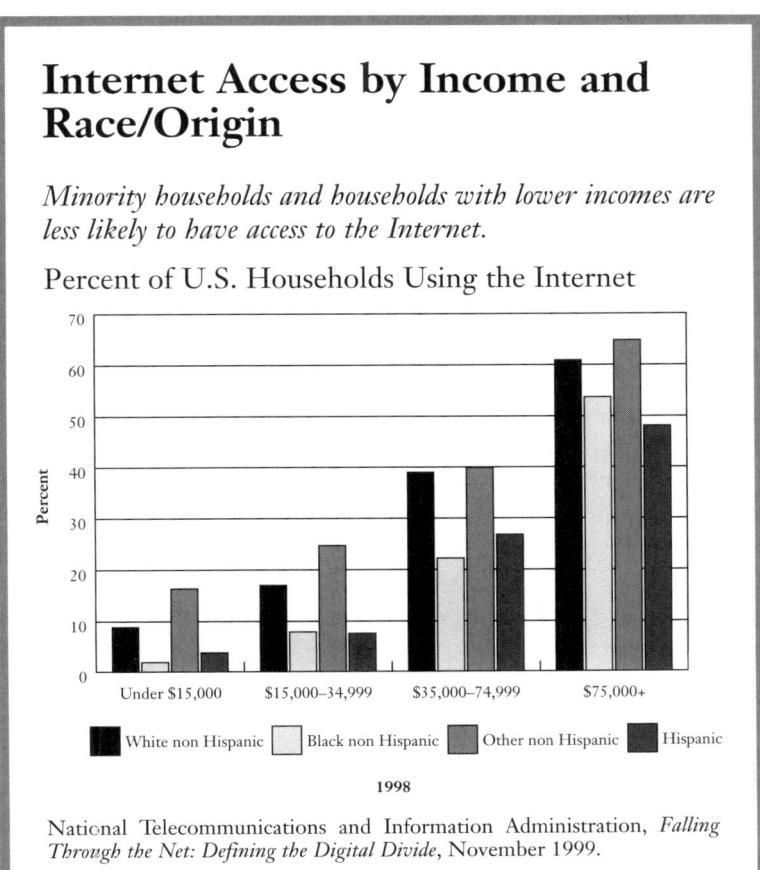

Internet Access by Income and Race/Origin

Minority households and households with lower incomes are less likely to have access to the Internet.

Percent of U.S. Households Using the Internet

1998

National Telecommunications and Information Administration, *Falling Through the Net: Defining the Digital Divide*, November 1999.

income households (e.g., the Federal Communications Commission's (FCC) Lifeline Assistance and Link-Up America; State programs) and support for high-cost regions of the country (e.g., the FCC's Universal Service Fund; other State and Federal rate-averaging) are prime examples of such programs. And the U.S. Department of Agriculture's Rural Utilities Service (RUS) provides targeted lending and technical advice to help ensure that advanced telecommunications infrastructure is in place for rural communities.

With the data in this report, we are in a better position to identify where and how to reach everyone. Policymakers should explore ways to continue to boost telephone penetration, particularly among the underserved, and to expand computer and Internet connectivity. For some individuals, it is an economic solution. Lower prices, leasing arrangements, and even free computer deals will bridge the digital gap for them. For high cost communities and low-income individuals, universal service policies will remain of critical importance. For other individuals, there are language and cultural barriers that need to be addressed. Products will need to be adapted to meet special needs, such as those of the disabled community. Finally, we need to redouble our outreach efforts, especially directed at the information disadvantaged.

Promoting Competition, Universal Service

To some extent, the surging use of computers and the Internet among American households reflects the success of our nation's pro-competition policies. A significantly higher percentage of households owned PCs in 1998 (42.1%) than in 1997 (36.6%), and experienced greater Internet access during the same period (26.2% versus 18.6%). The increased competition among PC-providers and lower costs of manufacturing have resulted in PCs selling for well below $1000. The increasing use of other Internet-accessing devices, such as televisions, palm computers, and Internet phones, should further invigorate competition among manufacturers and reduce prices for consumers.

While competition has made computers and the Internet increasingly affordable, these technologies still remain beyond the budget of many American households. When asked why they lacked Internet access, a significant portion of households

(16.8%) responded that it was too expensive. Respondents particularly cited the cost of monthly bills, followed by toll calling for Internet service provider (ISP) access. A significantly higher percentage of minority and low-income households reported that Internet access was cost prohibitive. In addition, cost ranked highest among reasons given by those who discontinued Internet use. And, the proportion of non-use would surely be higher still for those who do not yet own PCs or other Internet-access devices. Policymakers, such as the Federal-State Universal Service Joint Board, State Public Service Commissions, and the Federal Communications Commission should carefully consider these facts in their attempts to evaluate the new universal service and access needs.

These findings suggest that further competition and price reductions will be vital to making information tools affordable for most Americans. Going forward, it will be important to promote policies that directly enhance competition among companies manufacturing computers and other Internet devices, as well as among Internet service providers. Expanding competition in rural areas and central cities is particularly significant, as these areas lag behind the national averages for PC-ownership and household Internet access.

At the same time, the data demonstrate the need for continued universal service support for telephony, particularly in rural and other high-cost areas. And we need to encourage the buildout of broadband networks to rural and other underserved areas of our nation, so that all Americans can take full advantage of new information technologies and services.

Expanding Community Access Centers

Competition is a significant answer to providing affordable access to computers and the Internet, but it is not the total solution. It is highly unlikely that, in the foreseeable future, prices will fall to the point where most homes will have computers and Internet access. As a result, a digital divide may continue to exist at home between the information rich and the information poor. Given the great advantages accruing to those who have access, it is not economically or socially prudent to idly await the day when most, if not all, homes can claim connectivity. Part of the short-term answer lies in providing Internet access at community access centers (CACs), such as schools, libraries, and other public access facilities.

The 1998 data demonstrate why providing public access to the Internet at these external sources is critical. To begin with, these sources tend to be used by groups that lack Internet access at home or at work; chiefly, minorities, people earning lower incomes, those with lower education levels, and the unemployed. Households with incomes of less than $20,000 and Black households, for example, are twice as likely to get Internet access through a public library or community center than are households earning more than $20,000 or White households. Similarly, low-income households and households with lower education levels are obtaining access at schools at far higher rates.

Moreover, the same households that are using community access centers at higher rates are also using the Internet more often than other groups to find jobs or for educational purposes. CACs are, therefore, providing the very tools these groups need to advance economically and professionally.

The data support the continued funding of CACs by both industry and government. Industry has already come forward with significant assistance. Companies are supporting the creation of community technology centers, helping connect schools through "NetDays," and donating computers and software to schools and neighborhood centers. NTIA's Telecommunications and Information Infrastructure Assistance Program (TIIAP) has funded a number of pioneering CAC efforts. The U.S. Department of Education's new Community Technology Centers (CTC) program will enable the funding of CACs in economically distressed communities on a broader scale.

The 1998 data also underscore the importance of the [Clinton 1992–2000] Administration's efforts to ensure that all schools and libraries have affordable access to the Internet. Under the E-rate program, telecommunications carriers are providing eligible schools and libraries with a discounted rate for telecommunications services, internal connections among classrooms, and Internet access. As a result, the E-rate program is helping to connect more than 80,000 schools and libraries and is enabling children and adults to both learn new technologies and have new points of access. The data demonstrate that these community access centers are, indeed, used by people who lack access at home and merit further funding. In addition, we should look to other community-based organizations that can help us achieve these goals—traditional community centers, churches, credit unions, housing projects, senior centers, museums, fire and police stations, and more. Each community knows best how to reach and connect its residents.

Building Awareness

While many Americans are embracing computers and the Internet, there are many others who do not realize that this technology is relevant to their lives. We need to reach out to these communities and let them know why they should care—how new technologies can open new opportunities for them and their children.

We also need to find out *why* people are or are not connected. While such outreach works best at the local level, this type of information should be shared with policymakers at all levels of government—local, state, tribal, and federal. Only when we have a good understanding about why different communities do or do not have access to digital tools can we fashion appropriate policies. . . .

Good public policy requires a good factual foundation. Continued studies—public and private—are vital to permitting policymakers to make prudent decisions. Policymakers should explore ways to improve the availability of reliable penetration data for historically small but vitally important groups, such as Native Americans and Asians/Pacific Islanders. Potential solutions include "over-sampling" as part of a broader-based survey or conducting special studies that target these groups. A new analytical tool to gauge the status of Internet connectivity could be a Household Access Index (HAI), designed to highlight progress or deficiencies in this regard. A composite index could be developed that represents the country's combined penetration for telephones, computers, other Internet access devices, and the Internet. In 1998, the HAI for U.S. households would have equaled 162.4%, increasing from 149.0% in 1997.

In the final analysis, no one should be left behind as our nation advances into the 21st century, where having access to computers and the Internet may be key to becoming a successful member of society.

Computer Technology and the Right to Privacy

Gregory J.E. Rawlins

In dozens of ways every day, people create electronic files about themselves. Author Gregory J.E. Rawlins notes that bank and credit card transactions, visits to doctors' offices, insurance claims, and income tax filings are just a few of the ways in which people unwittingly funnel personal data into computer networks. Rawlins, an associate professor of computer science at Indiana University, says we live in a world driven by information, where the gathering and selling of facts about others has become a big business. Because of this troublesome and widespread sharing of computerized information, he believes people are losing control of their privacy.

IF I CAN IMPERSONATE YOU, I CAN DESTROY YOUR life. With the right identifiers, I can sign contracts in your name, empty your bank accounts, turn you into a bad credit risk, alter your health insurance, cancel your life insurance, and commit crimes in your name. To the systems that govern our lives, I become you.

Too Many Secrets

It used to be that locks and safes were enough to protect secrets and that the only ones seriously worried about them were spies, generals, and presidents. Not anymore. With the com-

■

puter's increasing use, secrecy systems have come to stay. Nowadays all communication is rapidly going electronic. Soon, virtually every communication act except face-to-face meetings will be electronic, and even they might be electronically bugged. The computer has led us to this impasse, but the computer isn't the problem. The problem is secrecy.

We are surrounded by too many secrets—secrets stored in and protecting information in hospitals, banks, insurance companies, communications networks, psychiatric wards, and police departments. They control access to restricted areas and school grades as well as to world currency transactions and nuclear weapons, stock exchanges, and voter-registration rolls. They govern the intimate workings of the government, the mint, the military, air traffic control, food distribution, and power stations. From transportation to energy, from food to currency, from weapons to prisons, breaking into secret systems can lead to smuggling; impersonation; industrial espionage; money laundering; sabotage; terrorism; and economic, military, and political power. Now that computers control weapon systems, secrecy systems have become as important as nuclear weapons. Which is why all governments guard knowledge of them so zealously.

Secrets in Computer Files

We all swim in an invisible sea of secrets. Visit a bank and you create a file; go to the doctor and you create a file; log on to a computer and you create a file. Transact any kind of business— or file an income tax return, or get counted in a census, or apply for a postal change of address—and you create many files. These files have long been with us, but with the computer's incursion many of the defenses that once protected them from prying eyes—whether the government's or our neighbors'— are gone, or fading fast. Making information electronic while leaving only the old-fashioned protections in place (doors, locks, safes, guns) simply makes it easier to get. . . .

Technology can protect us, but we have to know about it before we can clamor for it. Most of us today know nothing about it so we aren't requesting it from our leaders. In fact, if anything, the reverse is happening. Big business and governments know the value of information. They've been agitating for years to get at all those lovely facts. And so far they're winning.

Secrets from Big Brother

In 1948, when George Orwell published his novel *1984*, there were no computers to speak of—and he wasn't much of a technologist to begin with. But now Big Brother can hire all the technologists he wants. Despite recent setbacks in a few advanced countries, all police and spy agencies keep pushing for various anti-privacy laws, arguing that knowing everything about everybody is the only way for them to fight crime, terrorism, and subversion.

Well, they're right. But some fear that with such a system in place, nothing can protect us from unscrupulous government agents. Or perhaps even a police state. On the other hand, privacy as we in advanced countries understand it today is a modern invention. A hundred years ago nobody worried about privacy—protection against highway-men was more important. Having the sheriff know that bandits were nearby was far more important than having him know what kind of shoes we buy.

Today, however, those of us in advanced nations don't only have to worry about one potential Big Brother; there are already hundreds of thousands, perhaps millions, of Little Brothers. Now that electronic information about everyone and everything is publicly available, surveillance has branched out from its ancient roots in spying and become the province of big business, organized crime, and every computer-literate person. Indeed, readily available electronic information has grown to such massive quantities that a whole new profession is arising—that of *knowledge miner*. That's why many businesses are so busily collecting information.

Grocery Store Secrets

Many grocery stores, for example, are now trying to give their customers identification cards. Those cards seem to be like finding money in the street: use them and our grocery bills go down because we get special deals on certain items. In exchange, the store is gaining intimate knowledge about us and our shopping habits and, indirectly, everyone's shopping habits. Of course, if we use a credit or debit card the store doesn't have to give us a card of their own—we've already given them all that information for free. That information can be transmuted into money.

Nowadays [1996], there are an estimated five million electronic information bases worldwide, and the total volume of electronic information is doubling roughly every two years. It has already surpassed the amount of information stored on paper. By making such huge amounts of information available cheaply and quickly, and by letting anyone analyze that information, computers let us combine lots of previously useless information in new ways.

Addresses No Longer Secret

If you give me your phone number today, for example, you may also be giving me your address. In the old days I could only derive one from the other if I had lots of money. I would have had to pay an army to enter all the telephone numbers and addresses, buy high-priced computers, and hire even pricier programmers to organize and access that mass of information. Nobody but the ultrarich could do that; and they didn't need to do it because they could just hire detectives to follow you around.

But today, for just eighty dollars, I can buy two computer disks listing ninety million American homes and businesses. As soon as I know your telephone number, I also know your address. And the technology is getting cheaper by the minute.

If I know what I'm doing, here's how it might work today when you call me. Immediately I might see a map of where you live, with the location narrowed down to something like a block, or even a floor of a building. Because census information is already electronically available, I might get a feel for your neighborhood, your income level, perhaps your credit history, and so on. If motor vehicle information bases are tied in, I might learn your license plate number and registration, insurance premiums, and rate of renewal. Mail order companies and retail stores pool and sell their information; so I might also know about your annual expenditures, catalogs you receive, how much you spend on groceries, and all sorts of other things. You can learn a lot just by watching what people buy and where they live.

Perhaps you don't mind one person knowing your credit history; another knowing where you live; a third knowing when you're away on vacation; or a fourth knowing whether you're female, live alone, are elderly or ill, have ever taken self-defense classes, own a gun or dog, or have a home protection system. But if anyone can easily learn all those things just from your license number, credit card number, social security number—or even your phone number—you're simply fruit ripe for the picking.

Preserving Liberty and Secrets

> Liberty cannot be preserved without a general knowledge among the people. . . . The preservation of the means of knowledge among the lowest ranks is of more importance to the public than all the property of all the rich men.
>
> John Adams, *Dissertation on the Canon and Federal Law*

We have erected safeguards against anyone knowing how we vote because we've had thousands of years to experience what happens when we don't protect that information. We know that voting information can be easily misused, so we don't even let our own governments have it. Until now, however, we've had no such experience with letting anyone know what we buy, what we read, what we eat, what we do, how much we earn, where we live, what we think. Most of us, ignorant of privacy systems now available, give all that information away.

Information is money. If you know a little about many people, or a lot about some people, you can make more money than if you don't. Information is a commodity. It's something you can buy and sell, mine and refine, repackage and resell, just like any material resource. Now that the secret design of a company's next-generation product is worth far more than the raw materials needed to build it, information will become the oil and wheat and iron of the twenty-first century.

Power from Secrets

Information is also power—the strongest drug in the world. All governments run on wheels within wheels that they rarely let their own populace see. To protect reputations, to win elections, or simply through greed, career-minded officials have been known to bury damaging information. To gain a political edge, even friendly nations spy on each other; and to gain an economic edge, unfriendly nations arm each other. Power has always been a game of politics over justice, propaganda over truth, expediency over morality. Nations are no more moral than the people they represent.

Because many of us dislike hearing such things, all governments find it easier simply not to tell us. That pantomime practicality, that difference between what-we-say and what-we-do, creates and perpetuates the need for secrecy. It won't ever go away.

But while the game may not go away, technology can change its rules. Today's encryption technology could, if used widely enough, make us the last generation ever to have to fear for our privacy. On the other hand, if misused, it could make us the last generation with any notion of personal privacy at all. Our choices, it seems, are growing starker and starker. . . .

Our legal, governmental, and social systems are still designed for a world without computers. Our sluggish social systems, intended for the languid bygone era of only a decade ago—an era filled with filing cabinets, paper documents, and five-day mail—haven't changed to keep up. And computer technology keeps changing so fast now that perhaps they never will.

Virtual Reality vs. Real Life

Mark Slouka

Mark Slouka has taught writing at Columbia, Harvard, Penn State, and the University of Virginia. In his book *War of the Worlds: Cyberspace and the High-Tech Assault on Reality*, he challenges the assumption that technological advances are always good. In the book's introduction, excerpted below, Slouka voices his concern that the "virtual reality" of computers and the Internet could threaten the quality of people's genuine lives. For example, he believes that computer games that allow people to commit virtual violence may desensitize them to the real thing. On a broader scale, Slouka opposes technology enthusiasts who envision a future in which people spend more of their time in online virtual communities than they do in the real world. Caution is warranted, he concludes, because the constantly evolving technologies of the Internet and virtual reality could fundamentally change human behavior.

LET ME STATE MY CASE AS DIRECTLY AS POSSIBLE: I believe it is possible to see, in a number of technologies spawned by recent developments in the computer world, an attack on reality as human beings have always known it. I believe this process has been under way for some time, that it will be aided immeasurably by the so-called digital revolution currently sweeping through the industrialized world, and that its implications for our culture are enormous.

■

I'm the first to admit that this may seem an absurd contention. Most of us, after all, have little trouble separating reality from illusion. We know, for example, that Homer Simpson is a cartoon character on TV, while our neighbor, however much he may act like one, is not; that the highway during our morning commute, the sky at noon, or the bird on the wire at dusk, are not hallucinations; that a drawing of a two-by-four does not a two-by-four make.

Within a few years, however, distinctions such as these will be less automatic. We'll be able to pick up an electronically generated two-by-four. Feel its weight. Swing it around. Whack somebody with it. And yet none of it—not the two-by-four, the person we hit, or the landscape in which this takes place—will be real, in the usual, physical sense. We'll be able to immerse ourselves in an entirely synthetic world, a world that exists only as a trick of the senses, a computer-induced hallucination. And when we emerge from cyberspace—that strange nonplace beyond the computer screen—all indicators suggest that we will find it increasingly difficult to separate real life (already demoted to the acronym RL on computer Nets around the world) from virtual existence. Or worse, that we will know the difference but opt for the digitized world over the real one.

Technology Encroaches On Real

However futuristic all this may sound, it's not all that new. In May 1938, in an essay written for *Harper's Magazine*, E.B. White predicted the encroachment of technology on what we might call the territory of the real. "Clearly," he noted, "the race today is . . . between the things that are and the things that seem to be, between the chemist at RCA [Radio Corporation of America] and the angel of God." Already, he pointed out, sound effects had begun taking the place of sound itself. Television and radio were enlarging the eye's range, advertising an abstract place, an Elsewhere, that would grow to seem increasingly real. In time, he concluded *representations* of life, seen on radio and television and in the movies, would come to seem more lifelike to us than their originals.

White called it perfectly. Only months after his prediction, citizens up and down the Eastern seaboard of the United States were heading for the hills, panicked by Orson Welles's [American actor] radio adaptation of H.G. Wells's *War of the Worlds* into believing that sixteen-tentacled Martians had landed on Earth. It was a dramatic victory for the chemist at RCA and a defining moment for the New Age. For the thousands who rushed north to escape the Martians' onslaught, Welles's electronic illusion easily triumphed over common sense *and* reality.

The Digital Avant-Garde

The Martians (or the forces of electronic illusion) have been rolling on ever since. The war of the worlds—pitting physical reality against the forces of Elsewhere—continues, and reality continues to take it on the chin. In Yugoslavia recently, an actor who had portrayed the deceased dictator Marshal Tito in a docudrama found himself applauded, and reviled, by ordinary citizens on the streets of Belgrade. In Rio de Janeiro, when a soap opera villain murdered his co-star in real life, the actual homicide and the tortured plot of the *telenovela* fused seamlessly in the public mind. When the National Weather Service interrupted daytime programming to issue a tornado warning for a county in Kansas, the local TV station was flooded with phone calls from outraged citizens incensed over having to miss their soaps.

But television's transgressions on the territory of the real are just minor skirmishes compared to the all-out assault being conducted by the digital avant-garde. The race, you see, is no longer between the angel of God and the chemist at RCA. It's between the angel of God and the computer visionary at Microsoft. Or Apple. Or MIT. And he's not interested in imitating reality; he's out to replace it altogether. What the computer world is doing, says John Perry Barlow, Grateful Dead lyricist-turned-computer-cowboy, "is taking material and making it immaterial: Now is the flesh made word, in many respects."

Life as Computer Code

Reduced to its essentials, it comes down to this: only a decade after White's death [in 1985], we stand on the threshold of turning life itself into computer code, of transforming the experience of living in the physical world—every sensation, every detail—into a product for our consumption. "We now have the ability," says Barlow, "to take the sum of human experience and give it a medium in which to flow." What this means, simply, is that computer simulations may soon be so pervasive (and so realistic) that life itself will require some sort of mark of authenticity. Reality, in other words, may one day come with an asterisk.

None of which should come as much of a surprise. These, after all, are the days of miracle and wonder, of "telepresence" and "immersion technology" (which promise to submerge us in a fully sensual, synthetic world), of intelligent software, artificial life, and virtual damn-near everything. Entire virtual communities, some numbering ten thousand citizens and more, are now accessible through the conceptual window of your computer screen. Many have homes, prostitutes, tree houses for your children. Within five years, according to John Quarterman, a cyberspace cartographer, the digital world will be inhabited by over a billion individuals worldwide. Those of us still on the outside, Professor Timothy Ferris of Berkeley informs us, will be able to "watch grandmothers be shot by snipers in Sarajevo from six camera angles" without leaving our couches. . . .

Technology Is a Powerful Force

Technology is never a neutral force: it orders our behavior, redefines our values, reconstitutes our lives in ways we can't always predict. Like a political constitution or a legislative act, as Langdon Winner, professor of political science at Rensselaer Polytechnic Institute, has noted, technology establishes the rules by which people live. The digital revolution is technology with a capital T. And its rules, I suspect, may not be to everyone's liking.

Given the enormous effect the digital revolution may come to have on our lives (the digerati, as Steve Lohr [technology reporter for the *New York Times*] has called them, routinely liken its impact to that of the splitting of the atom, the invention of the Gutenberg Press, and the discovery of fire), there is something downright eerie about the lack of debate, the conspicuous absence of dissenting voices, the silence of the critics. Congress seems uninterested; watchdog groups sleep. Like shined deer, we seem to be wandering en masse onto the digital highway, and the only concern heard in the land, by and large, is that some of us may be left behind. Under the circumstances, some caution is surely in order, particularly if we consider that the digital revolution is having its greatest effect on the young. . . .

Concern for Consequences

My gripe, I should point out, is not so much with the technologies themselves as with the general lack of concern over the consequences that many new applications may come to have. I'm a humanist, not a Luddite [one who resists technology]. Though I'll admit to a certain fondness for old-fashioned pastimes (I'll take a book or a musical instrument over a Mac and a modem), I'm not incapable of appreciating the contemporary wonders—from gene splicing to lasers—that everywhere crowd in on our attention. I'm not insensitive to the benefits and beauties of technology; without them, my wife and my son would have died during childbirth.

So let me be as clear as possible: I have no problem with what Andrew S. Grove, president and CEO of the Intel Corporation, has called "the ubiquitous PC." I own and use one. Nor do I have any argument, for example, with the millions of people who crowd the "chat groups" available on the Net (many of whom I've found to be no more or less decent and interesting than people in the real world). My quarrel is with a relatively small but disproportionately influential group of self-described "Net religionists" and "wannabe gods" who believe that the physical world can (and should) be "downloaded" into a computer, who believe that the future of mankind is not in RL (real life) but in some form of VR (virtual reality); who are working very hard (and spending enormous amounts of both federal and private money) to engineer their very own version of the apocalypse. As intelligent as they are single-minded, these people have been ignored by the majority of humanists for too long; it's time we started listening.

Technology May Change Humanity

The *real* issue here, as the novelist and technoevangelist Robert Coover has pointed out, is how we answer the question, "What's human?" For some, he explains, humanity "has to do with souls and 'depth' and the search for meaning and purpose; with tradition, ritual, mystery and individualism." For others, like himself, it has more to do with the spiritualism of the hive: the increasingly interlinked system of computers and computer technologies about to subsume (as Kevin Kelly, the executive editor of *Wired* magazine, recently put it) the "millions of buzzing, dim-witted personal computers" (that's us) into one grand organism/machine immeasurably greater than the sum of its parts. For Coover (as for others, including Speaker of the House of Representatives [1995–1998] Newt Gingrich), our "evolution" into this hive state is inevitable. "I regret," he says, "having to give up the comforting fairy tales of the past: I, too, want to be unique, significant, connected to a 'deeper truth,' canonized. I want to *have* an 'I.' Too bad."

Of course, shedding "fairy tales" like tradition, individualism, and identity, Coover admits, may have its downside. "If creatures of the past were hived under queen bees like Alexander the Great or Genghis Khan," he points out (quite reasonably, I think), "it seems unlikely that hived creatures of the future will escape their own hive-masters." And what, one might wonder, will happen to the "unhived"? "No doubt they will get stepped on," says Coover; "the Sophist principle 'knowledge is power' will make them mere meat at the fringe." . . .

People May Become Insignificant

When a significant number of powerful individuals—scientists, academics, authors, engineers, computer programmers—following the scent of a potential $3.5 *trillion* industry begin referring to the human body as meat (the expression is a common one among the digerati), it's time for those still foolishly attached to theirs to start paying attention. When a subculture of enthusiasts yearning for the technological equivalent of rapture begins labeling the unhived (in a weak attempt at digital wit) PONAs (people of no account), the PONAs may want to start asking what counts and what doesn't.

"When the yearning for human flesh has come to an end," asks Barlow, referring to the human touch, not to cannibalism, "what will remain?" Good question. "Mind," he says hopefully, "may continue, uploaded into the Net, suspended in an ecology of voltage as ambitiously capable of self-sustenance as was that of its carbon-based forebears." To unhived PONAs like myself, this is hardly encouraging. I *like* my carbon-based body and the carbon-based bodies of my wife and children and friends. I like my carbon-based dog and my carbon-based garden. Nor, to pick up on Coover's "meat on the fringe" image, do I particularly fancy myself as roadkill on the digital highway. . . .

Coover and Co. may find my timidity quaint, my values hopelessly sentimental. I can live with that. What it comes down to, it seems to me, is this: human culture depends on the shared evidence of the senses, always has; we can communicate with one another because a hurled rock will always break skin, a soap bubble always burst. A technology designed to short-circuit the senses, a technology capable of providing an alternate world—abstract, yet fully inhabitable, real to our senses yet accessible only through a computer screen—would take away this common ground and replace it with one manufactured for us by the technologists.

Ethics Based in Reality

And this is not a good thing. Why? Because human history, in the largest sense, has been the record of our debate with the world. Because reality has been and continues to be the great touchstone for the world's ethical systems. Because, simply put, the world provides context, and without context, ethical behavior is impossible. It is the physical facts of birth and pain and pleasure and death that force us (enable us) to make value judgments: *this* is better than *that*. Nourishment is better than hunger. Compassion is better than torture. Virtual systems, by offering us a reality divorced from the world, from the limits and responsibilities of presence, offer us as well a glimpse into an utterly amoral universe. Consider an obvious example: in Night Trap, a CD-ROM video game recently popular among prepubescent boys, vampires drill holes into the necks of their barely clad female victims and hang them from meat hooks; virtual reality (coming soon to a modem near you) will allow you to *be* the vampire. To inflict pain. Without responsibility. Without consequences. The punctured flesh will heal at the touch of a button, the scream disappear into cyberspace. You'll be able to resurrect the digital dead and kill them again.

The implications of these new technologies are social; the

questions they pose, broadly ethical; the risks they entail, unprecedented. They are the cultural equivalent of genetic engineering, except that in this experiment, even more than in the other one, *we* will be the potential new hybrids, the two-pound mice.

The Effects Are Still Unknown

What will technologies that alter our sense of reality mean, in the long run? What will they do to us? No one knows. Ask the technovisionaries how human beings (who have evolved over millions of years in response to the constraints and pressures of the physical world) might respond to existence in aphysical environments, or to the wholesale cyberization of the human environment, and they'll fall over one another in their willingness to admit that they have no idea. Does this concern them just a little? Frighten them, maybe? Not a bit. "The best things in life are scary," Kevin Kelly told me recently, "I'm serious." Unfortunately for the rest of us, he probably is. So on we go, blindfolded, pedal to the floor, over the canyonlands. . . .

I am no Oliver Stone [a movie director]. I have no interest in conspiracy theories. Nor do I wish to gloss over the very real benefits the digital New Age may bring; technology, as I have said, is never a wholly one-sided affair. My concern, rather, is based on a small number of well-worn truths: that the free market can unleash forces difficult to control; that technological innovation has its own logic, often separate from questions of value and ethics; and that *some* technologies—particularly those that promise (or threaten) to transform human culture as we know it—bear watching.

The Internet as a Cause of Social Isolation

John Markoff

Early in 2000, the Stanford Institute for the Quantitative Study of Society released its report *Internet and Society*. The study concluded that the Internet—which people use alone—might be creating feelings of isolation among those who go online. If the Internet causes people to spend substantially less time in real human contact, it might have negative social consequences. The article below, written by *New York Times* reporter John Markoff, offers both a discussion of the institute's findings and comments from those who disagree with the study.

THE NATION'S OBSESSION WITH THE INTERNET is causing many Americans to spend less time with friends and family, less time shopping in stores and more time working at home after hours, according to one of the first large-scale surveys of the societal impact of the Internet.

In short, "the more hours people use the Internet, the less time they spend with real human beings," said Norman Nie, a political scientist at Stanford University who was the principal investigator for the study.

A Wave of Social Isolation

Mr. Nie asserted that the Internet was creating a broad new wave of social isolation in the United States, raising the specter

■

of an atomized world without human contact or emotion.

That conclusion is certain to prove controversial because some online enthusiasts contend that the Internet has fostered alternative electronic relationships that may replace or even enhance face-to-face family and social connections.

"This is not a zero-sum game," said Howard Rheingold, author of "Virtual Community: Homesteading on the Electronic Frontier." "People's social networks do not consist only of people they see face to face. In fact, social networks have been extending because of artificial media since the printing press and the telephone."

The Stanford survey, which was conducted by the university's Institute for the Quantitative Study of Society and will be published on Wednesday [February 16, 2000] appears to offer an Internet-era parallel to some of the findings of "The Lonely Crowd," a landmark sociological analysis of American society in 1950.

The book, written by David Riesman with Nathan Glazer and Reuel Denney, described the changing American character and chronicled the shift away from family and community-centered life and the ascendance of mass media.

The Stanford study, in turn, details how the Internet is leading to a rapid shift away from mass media. The study reported that 60 percent of regular Internet users said they had reduced their television viewing, and one-third said they spent less time reading newspapers.

Those regular users, spending at least five hours a week online, represented about 20 percent of those surveyed and were the group looked at most closely. In all, the study found that 55 percent of those polled had Internet access at home or work and that 43 percent of households were online.

And the study found evidence that the Internet was allowing the workplace to invade the home. A quarter of regular Internet users employed at least part time said the Internet had increased the time they spent working at home without reducing the time spent at work.

The Importance of Human Contact

In the past Mr. Nie has been the author of studies on the decline of American involvement in political and community or-

Stanford Study Biased

Many in the media offered rebuttals to the Stanford Institute study that concluded Internet use causes feelings of social isolation. Below, regular BYTE.com columnist Fred Langa asserts that the Stanford researchers revealed a personal bias against new technology.

The study has all the normal trappings of objectivity and statistical validity, but to me, it appears the researchers' interpretation of the results is rooted in a subtle, but distinct anti-Web/anti-tech bias. This is especially disturbing in light of the wide play the survey got in the national media. . . .

[The researchers] appear to regard e-mail as a socially inferior medium. For example, in a press release about the study, one researcher says, "E-mail is a way to stay in touch, but you can't share a coffee or a beer with somebody on e-mail or give them a hug."

OK. But you can't share a coffee or a beer or a hug by telephone, either. So, wouldn't it stand to reason that the more time we spend on the phone, the more socially isolated we are? (Huh?) And you know, you also can't share a coffee or a beer or a hug by snail mail, so every time you send someone a card or a letter, you're merely increasing your social isolation, right? Clearly, there's something wrong with this thinking, and I think the clue to what the flaw is can be found in the same press release where one of the researchers says, "For the most part, the Internet is an individual activity." But the study says that e-mail is the No.1 Internet activity. That's "individual" only if you see one end of the connection, or only if you somehow come to believe that in communicating online, you're interacting with your computer rather than with your correspondents.

Fred Langa, "Is the Web Isolating You? Stanford Study Says 'Yes,'" *BYTE.com*, May 22, 2000.

ganizations. He said that while much of the public Internet debate had been focused on the invasion of privacy, little study had been done of the potential psychological and emotional impact of what he said would be more people "home, alone and anonymous."

Mr. Nie, a co-author of the study with Prof. Lutz Erbring of the Free University of Berlin, contended that there was no evidence that virtual communities would provide a substitute for traditional human relationships.

"If I go home at 6:30 in the evening and spend the whole night sending e-mail and wake up the next morning, I still haven't talked to my wife or kids or friends," Mr. Nie said. "When you spend your time on the Internet, you don't hear a human voice and you never get a hug."

The new study was based on a sample of 4,113 adults in 2,689 households. It is the second major research project to suggest that the advent of the Internet may have negative social consequences.

Carnegie Study Also Found Loneliness

In August 1998 researchers at Carnegie Mellon University reported that people who spent even a few hours a week connected to the Internet experienced higher levels of depression and loneliness.

In contrast to the Carnegie Mellon study, which focused on psychological and emotional issues, the Stanford survey is an effort to provide a broad demographic picture of Internet use and its potential impact on society.

"No one is asking the obvious questions about what kind of world we are going to live in when the Internet becomes ubiquitous," Mr. Nie said.

"No one asked these questions with the advent of the automobile, which led to unplanned suburbanization, or with the rise of television, which led to the decline of our political parties."

"We hope we can give society a chance to talk through some of these issues before the changes take place," he said.

Americans overwhelmingly use e-mail as their most common Internet activity, according to the Stanford researchers.

Moreover, the report found that most Internet users treated the network as a giant public library, albeit with a commercial tilt.

Despite the general perception that the Internet has become a vast cybernetic shopping mall, the Stanford study indicates that only 25 percent of the Internet users surveyed make purchases online and that fewer than 10 percent do other types of financial transactions online, like banking.

Some Dispute Stanford Findings

Some critics strongly disagree with the researchers' assertion that the Internet is leading to a new form of social isolation.

"It's true by definition that if you're spending more hours hitting the keyboard you're not spending time with other people," said Amatai Etzioni, a sociologist at George Washington University. "But people do form very strong relations over the Internet, and many of them are relations that they could not find any other way."

Mr. Nie disagrees, arguing that today's patterns of Internet usage foretell a loss of interpersonal contact that will result in the kind of isolation seen among many elderly Americans.

"There are going to be millions of people with very minimal human interaction," he said. "We're really in for some things that are potentially great freedoms but frightening in terms of long-term social interaction."

Pornography, Hate Groups, and Censorship of the Internet

Seydou Amadou Oumarou and René Lefort

Some of the most lamented aspects of the Internet are that it makes pornography available to anyone who goes online and provides racists and other hate groups with a forum to espouse their views. In 1995 public concern over online pornography resulted in the Communications Decency Act (CDA), a federal law that made it illegal to use the Net to display or send "indecent" material that could be seen by a minor. In 1997 the U.S. Supreme Court ruled the CDA violated the First Amendment right to free speech and was therefore unconstitutional.

However, many parents, politicians, and pundits wonder how effective the CDA would have been even if it had not been struck down by the Court. The Internet links over 100 million people in many countries, each with their different views of what material is "indecent" and whether such material should be censored. In the article excerpted below, writers Seydou Amadou Oumarou and René Lefort of the United Nations Educational, Scientific, and Cultural Organization (UNESCO) discuss the many difficulties that national governments wishing to censor the Internet face.

∎

Excerpted from "The Web, the Spider, and the Fly," by Seydou Amadou Oumarou and René Lefort, *UNESCO Courier*, September 1998. Reprinted with permission.

A SKULL ROTATES ON THE BLACK SCREEN. THE picture of a baby flanked by Hitler's moustache or a photomontage of Arnold Schwarzenegger wielding a sword with [actress] Ingrid Bergman at his feet, both of them naked, file past. This sort of thing may amuse some people, but it is no laughing matter when sites on bomb-making, child prostitution and the superiority of the white race appear. The Internet, the outcome of a successful marriage between telecommunications and information technology, is posing unprecedented information control problems which governments, service providers, educators and families are finding hard to solve.

A newspaper has an editorial team and a printing plant, a television network has newscasters, studios and transmitters. In other words, traditional media are identifiable and have a physical or material component that the authorities can call to account when they consider that the law has been broken. They can prosecute a journalist, shut down a newspaper or confiscate a transmitter. The media are also attached to a territory. Their messages may cross borders, but their activities come under the jurisdiction of at least one country.

Can the World Monitor the Internet?

The Internet is another matter altogether. First of all, there are countless transmitters of information. A hundred million people have access to the Internet, and any one of them can not only send electronic mail and take part in chat forums but, with a little electronic tinkering, turn their personal computer into a service provider that others can tap into. In a way, that person then becomes "virtual." His or her message can travel along so many routes that when it reaches its destination, the original source can no longer be traced.

Legitimate or not, the monitoring of contents must take this new situation into account. That would require a universal agreement based on a common set of ethics, or at least a lowest common denominator. But that is far from the case. The Netherlands, China, Zambia, the United States, Cuba and France, to name just a few countries, have radically different and even irreconcilable views on what is and what is not permissible on the Internet.

Internet service providers and some organizations campaigning to "clean up the Web" point to an assault on morality. The fierce competition among service providers has led many of them to cultivate a wholesome image on issues such as paedophilia, which strikes a chord in public opinion, out of fear of being considered purveyors of "smut."

In The Netherlands, the authorities have no intention of passing repressive laws. Instead they are encouraging service providers to clean up their act by eliminating paedophile and racist sites from their servers. In January 1996 Dutch Internet service providers created a foundation in charge of tracking down undesirable sites. Law enforcement officials step in only when the author of the incriminating pages refuses to comply. But Renee Zwart, a member of the foundation who believes censorship is a "medieval instrument," says her organization does not attack freedom of expression.

Tools Can Screen Out Undesirable Sites

Many companies supply their clients with tools to screen out pornographic and racist sites. Several such programs are on the market, including Cyber Patrol, CYBERsitter, NetNanny and Surfwatch. They offer a list of websites or forums with a reputation for containing material considered offensive and a list of key words that are judged obscene. The connection is interrupted whenever a user tries to log on to one of these sites or as soon as a forbidden word appears on screen. The Electronic Frontier Foundation, an American organization dedicated to a radical defense of freedom of speech on the Internet, is totally in line with its country's laws and tradition. The foundation argues that although these programs screen out indecent content, they also block access to many political and social sites, including pages devoted to fighting AIDS and promoting women's rights. The experiment is "inconclusive." Moreover, "It is relatively easy to outsmart these programs, even for a beginner," says Jean-Paul Cloutier, an independent World Wide Web pioneer in Quebec and editor of *Chroniques de Cyberie* [Chronicles of Cyberspace], an on-line information and commentary magazine about the information highways.

Government restrictions can be enforced in the name of morality, but above all they are used to prevent the use of the Internet for "subversive" ends. In China, for example, Internet users must register with the police and agree not to use the medium for "antigovernment activities." What's more, the government, which has every modem owner on file, has monitored all traffic since 1996. "For example, it is now against the law for a businessman to use the Internet to obtain stock market information considered strategic," says Christophe Tronche, a member of the French section of Citadel, an organization that campaigns for the upholding of individual freedom on the Internet. In Cuba, the regulation commission, which approves requests for Internet access, is entirely made up of representatives of the justice, interior and armed forces ministries.

In countries like China and Cuba, monitoring cyberspace is easier because "the telecommunications operators belong to the state," Cloutier explains. But monitoring is less straightforward when the site is offered by a server located outside the country. That is the case, for example, in Algeria, where Internet users have access to a site created by "dissident officers" in the armed forces. "The Algerian government doesn't like our site's content. . . . We use the Web as an opportunity," says the site's anonymous webmaster.

Reporters Without Frontiers Defends Freedoms

The Internet can be used as an alternative to censored traditional media, especially the printed word. In November 1997 the French organization Reporters without Frontiers, which defends freedom of the press, tried using the Internet to give a new lease on life to the Mauritanian newspaper *Mauritanie Nouvelle* [New Mauritania], whose publication had been suspended for seven months, by putting some of the publication's articles online. Today, opponents of monolithic regimes can use the Internet to set up areas of freedom that are forbidden in their own countries and can reach an international audience that would be difficult to obtain otherwise. Censors around the world are coming up against this phenomenon because "right now the Internet is the only area of freedom outside all political control," says Lyonnel Thouvenot of Reporters without Frontiers.

In liberal democracies, where most efforts to ban material on the Internet are focused on sites with paedophile and racist content, the first attempt to control the Web dates back to 1995. That is when the U.S. Congress passed the Communication Decency Act, which aimed to severely punish the transmission of "shocking" and "indecent" material through computer networks in the name of the protection of children. Under the terms of the law, violators could face fines of up to $250,000 and two-year prison sentences. A year later the act was ruled unconstitutional and struck down by the Supreme Court. In the name of freedom of expression, neo-Nazi sites have also been allowed to continue in the United States and to flourish in Denmark.

In Germany last May [1998], a Munich court convicted Felix Somm, the former local manager of the service provider CompuServe, of spreading pornographic material over the Internet through newsgroups, handing down a suspended two-year prison sentence and fining him 100,000 marks [about $50,000]. The conviction has been appealed. The judicial authorities in Germany are also uncompromising when it comes to neo-Nazi propaganda or far-left on-line magazines such as *Radikal* [Radical], which is accused of being an apologist for violence. A Dutch server offers the periodical, which is also banned from newsstands. However, Cloutier says, "few states have laws specifically pertaining to the Internet. . . . Everything depends on how existing laws on freedom of expression are applied, on the margin of manoeuvre one had to criticize the government, on the national definitions of content that could endanger state security. . . ."

Encryption Technology Controls Information

The matter becomes even more complicated if encryption is taken into account. The main way in which the flow of information on the Internet is controlled is by states refusing to make encryption technology totally available. Encryption technology is based on a kind of lock that can be opened by a key known only to the two correspondents and makes it possible to read messages that were sent in code. Ending that monopoly would technically mean ending censorship on the Internet because anyone would be able to send or receive an encrypted message that no unauthorized person would be able to read. In fact, every state fears that these massive, repeated, cross-border electronic exchanges, which escape all control, will limit their powers and privileges in the age of globalization. Some of these powers are legitimate if they help combat money-laundering or the spread of paedophilia. Others are obsolete. The growth of electronic trade requires total protection of payment methods, which themselves depend on secure encryption. But most experts agree that the Internet must move out of its present primitive stage, in which scholars and "plugged-in" individuals exchange information, and become an instrument of mass commercial communication, whether it is used by companies between themselves, by producers, or by consumers.

Organizations that defend freedom of expression on the Internet, such as the American Civil Liberties Union (ACLU) and the Electronic Frontier Foundation (EFF), are fighting for the total availability of encryption technology, especially Pretty Good Privacy (PGP). This software may be available to all Internet users in the United States, but only in a version that is also in the possession of law enforcement officials. In France, encryption is done with special permission from the government so that the police can read the information.

There's no escaping one's roots. The military designed the Internet because it wanted a communications network with so many ramifications that the system wouldn't be paralysed by destroying one of its parts. Just try keeping tabs on that.

EXAMINING POP CULTURE

The Future
of High
Technology

The Age of Robots

Raymond Kurzweil

An inventor of computer-related technologies, Raymond Kurzweil notes that robots have often been portrayed as mechanical creatures prone to turning on their creators. In reality, they are sophisticated helpers. From the 1970s through the 1990s, robots have evolved from machines with limited arm and grasping movements to automated beings that can do such things as shear sheep, disarm mines in the Persian Gulf, and work in operating rooms and in the dangerous zones of nuclear power plants. They can read and play music and help the paralyzed care for themselves. In March 2000, Kurzweil received the National Medal of Technology—the nation's highest technology honor. He predicts that the tireless, strong, fast, and precise robot will become an increasingly familiar figure in homes and businesses.

IN *R.U.R.*, A PLAY WRITTEN IN 1921, THE CZECH dramatist Karel Capek (1890–1938) describes the invention of intelligent mechanical machines intended as servants for their human creators. Called robots, they end up disliking their masters and take matters into their own "hands." After taking over the world, they decide to tear down all symbols of human civilization. By the end of the play they have destroyed all of mankind. Although Capek first used the word "robot" in his 1917 short story "Opilec," creating the term from the Czech words "robota," meaning obligatory work, and "robotnik," meaning serf, *R.U.R.* (for "Rossum's Universal Robots") introduced the word into popular usage. Capek intended his intelligent machines to be evil in their perfection, their ultimate rationality scornful of human frailty. Although a mediocre play, it struck a chord by articulating the uneasy relationship between man and machine and achieved wide success on two continents. The spectre of machine intelligence enslaving its creators, or at least competing with human intelligence for employment and other privileges, has continued to impress itself on the public consciousness.

Early "Robots"

Although lacking human charm and good will, Capek's robots brought together all of the elements of machine intelligence: vision, auditory perception, touch sensitivity, pattern recognition, decision making, judgement, extensive world knowledge, fine motor coordination for manipulation and locomotion, and even a bit of common sense. The robot as an imitation or substitute for a human being has remained the popular conception. The first generation of modern robots was, however, a far cry from this anthropomorphic vision. The Unimation 2000, the most popular of the early "robots," was capable only of moving its arm in several directions and opening and closing its gripper. It had no senses and could move its arm with only two or three degrees of freedom (directions of movement) of the six possible in three-dimensional space. Typical applications of these early robots, introduced during the 1970s, involved moving objects from one place to another (a capability called pick and place).

More sophisticated devices, such as the American company Cincinnati Milacron's T3 (The Tomorrow Tool), the German KUKA robots, and the Japanese Hitachi robots, were introduced in the early 1980s. These second-generation robots can move with five or six degrees of freedom, can effect more precise movements, are faster, and have more delicate grippers. The motions of these robots can be programmed, but they still had no provision for conditional execution, that is, operations conditioned on some external event. Since these robots still have no way of sensing their environment, there are no inputs on which to base any decision making. These second-generation robots became well known for welding and spray painting, primarily in the automotive industry.

Third Generation Robots

The third generation, introduced in the mid 1980s, began to display a modicum of intelligence. Robots of this generation—Unimation's PUMA, IBM's 7535 and 7565, and Automatix's RAIL series—contain general-purpose computers integrated with vision and/or tactile sensing systems. By 1987 robotic vision systems alone had developed into a $300 million industry, with estimates of $800 million for 1990. Specialized programming languages, such as Unimation's VAL and IBM's AML, allow these robots to make decisions based on changes in their environment Such systems can, for example, find industrial parts regardless of their orientation and identify and use them appropriately in complex assembly tasks.

With the flexibility and sophistication of robots improving each year, the population of industrial robots has increased from a few hundred in 1970 to several hundred thousand by the late 1980s. Some are used in factories that are virtually to-

Movie Robots Reflect Changing Cultural Views

Robots made their first appearance on the silver screen in *Metropolis* (1926), Fritz Lang's bleak look at the future of the industrial revolution. The next significant robot didn't appear until the release of *Forbidden Planet* (1956), which introduced Robby the Robot, a huge whirring robot that's smarter than anyone else in the movie.

The drones in *Silent Running* (1971) can't talk, but they do express fear and sadness. The loyal droids in *Star Wars* (1977) brought some comedy to the screen and inspired generations of kids to want their own C-3POs.

The robots in Woody Allen's *Sleeper* (1973) were solely for comic relief: robot butlers serve drinks during a police raid, a seriously disheveled robot dog can only intone "Hello, my name is Rags," and two robot Jewish tailors can't fit a suit.

tally automated, such as Allen Bradley's facility for manufacturing electric motor starters. The only human beings in this factory monitor the process from a glass booth, while computers control the entire flow of work from electronically dispatched purchase orders to shipped products. Though the era of workerless factories has begun, the most significant short-term impact of this latest generation of robots is in settings where they work alongside human coworkers. Increasingly, new factories are designed to incorporate both human and machine assemblers, with the flow of materials monitored and controlled by computers.

Robots Can Do More

With the arrival of the third generation, the diversity of tasks being accomplished by robots has broadened considerably. A robot named Oracle is shearing sheep in western Australia. One called RM3 is washing, debarnacling, and painting the

As robotic technology advanced, robots were depicted as having more humanlike characteristics. In *Westworld* (1973), human replicas interact with guests in a $1,000-a-day amusement park—but then their circuits go haywire and they kill everyone. The genetically engineered robots in *Blade Runner* (1981) are like people, only stronger and smarter, and with only a four-year life span. In the end, they appreciate life more than the supposed humans.

Robots in film have become less complex in the age of big-budget movies. The *Terminator* cyborgs (1984, 1991) don't think or feel . . . they just shoot. But who needs depth with those kinds of action sequences and special effects? There could be hope for smart robots next summer [2001], however, when Steven Spielberg's *A.I.* ("artificial intelligence") is due to be released.

Lisa Kalis, "Lights! Robots! Action!" *Red Herring*, August 2000.

hulls of ships in France. Several dozen brain operations have been performed at Long Beach Memorial Hospital in California with the help of a robot arm for precision drilling of the skull. In 1986 police in Dallas used a robot to break into an apartment in which a suspect had barricaded himself. The frightened fugitive ran out of the apartment and surrendered. The U.S. Defense Department is using undersea robots built by Honeywell to disarm mines in the Persian Gulf and other locations. Thousands of robots are routinely used in bioengineering laboratories to perform the extremely delicate operations required to snip and connect minute pieces of DNA. And walking robots are used in nuclear power plants to perform operations in areas too dangerous for humans. One such robot, Odetics's Odex, looks like a giant spider with its six legs.

The next generation of robots will take several more steps in replicating the subtlety of human perceptual ability and movement, while retaining a machine's inherent advantages in speed, memory, precision, repeatability, and tireless operation. Specialized chips are being developed that will provide the massively parallel computations required for a substantially higher level of visual perception. Equally sophisticated tactile sensors are being designed into robot hands. Manipulators with dozens of degrees of freedom will combine the ability to lift both very heavy objects and delicate ones without breaking the latter. These robots' "local" intelligence will be fully integrated into the computerized control systems of a modern factory.

Robots Compete with Humans

Forerunners of these robots of the 1990s are beginning to compete with human dexterity and intelligence on many fronts. A robot developed by Russell Anderson of Bell Labs can defeat most human opponents at Ping-Pong. Two other Ping-Pong playing robots, one English and one Japanese, recently met each other in San Francisco for a match. A robot hand developed at the University of Utah can crack an egg, drop the contents into a mixing bowl, and then whip up an omelette mixture all at several times the speed of a master chef. The Stanford/JPL Hand, designed by Kenneth Salisbury and other MIT researchers, is a three-fingered robot that can perform such intricate tasks as turning a wing nut. A collaborative effort now underway between the University of Utah Center for Biomedical Design and the MIT Artificial Intelligence Laboratory aims at constructing a hand that will "exhibit performance levels roughly equivalent to the natural human hand," according to Stephen Jacobsen, the chief designer of the project. A voice-activated robot to provide quadriplegic patients such personal services as shaving, brushing teeth, feeding and retrieving food and drinks is being developed by Larry Leifer and Stefan Michalowski under a grant from the Veterans Administration. . . .

U.S. Defense Uses Robots

Not surprisingly, the world's largest supporter of robotic research is the U.S. Defense Department, which foresees a wide range of roles for robotic fighters in the 1990s and early twenty-first century. A walking truck with fat bent legs is being developed by the U.S. Army for roadless terrains. The U.S. Air Force is developing a number of pilotless aircraft, or flying robots, that can perform a variety of reconnaissance and attack missions. Early versions of such robot craft played a vital role in the Israeli destruction of 29 Russian surface-to-air missile (SAM) sites in the Bekaa Valley in a single hour during its invasion of Lebanon in 1982.

The field of robotics is where all of the AI [artificial intelligence] technologies meet: vision, pattern recognition, knowledge engineering, decision-making, natural-language understanding, and others. As the underlying technologies mature and as the growing corps of robot designers gets better at integrating these diverse technologies, robots will become increasingly ubiquitous. They will tend our fields and livestock, build our products, assist our surgeons; eventually they will even help us clean our houses. This last task has turned out to be one of the most difficult. As we have seen with other AI problems, machine intelligence has first been successfully deployed in situations where unpredictable events are held to a minimum. It was not surprising, therefore, that manufacturing was the first successful application for robotic technology, since factories can be designed to provide predictable and relatively well-organized environments for robots to work in. In contrast, the environments of our homes change rapidly and present many unpredictable obstacles. So, effective robotic servants in the home will probably not appear until early in the next [twenty-first] century. By that time, however, robotic technology will have dramatically transformed the production and service sectors of society.

Expecting More from Computers

Neil Gershenfeld

Best-selling author Neil Gershenfeld asserts that the digital revolution has definitely favored computers and not the people who use them. Computer gurus describe computers with endless speed, Internet entertainment, and learning that is only a click away. But for the ordinary person, writes Gershenfeld, computers are still frustrating boxes that do not enhance life. Gershenfeld, who leads the Physics and Media Group at the Massachusetts Institute of Technology Media Lab and directs the Things That Think research consortium, believes people should expect more from their computers. He concludes that these machines should work harder to do what people want and to perform their tasks as easily and invisibly as possible.

TO A SPECIES THAT SEEKS TO COMMUNICATE, offering instantaneous global connectivity is like wiring the pleasure center of a rat's brain to a bar that the rat then presses over and over until it drops from exhaustion. I hit bottom when I found myself in Corsica, at the beach, in a pay phone booth, connecting my laptop with an acoustic modem coupler to take care of some perfectly mundane e-mail. That's when I threw away my pager that delivered e-mail to me as I traveled, disconnected my cell phone that let my laptop download e-mail anywhere, and began answering e-mail just once a day. These technologies were like the rat's pleasure bar, just capable

■

enough to provide instant communication gratification, but not intelligent enough to help me manage that communication.

Digital Reality

The Digital Revolution has promised a future of boundless opportunity accessed at the speed of light, of a globally wired world, of unlimited entertainment and education within everyone's reach. The digital reality is something less than that.

The World Wide Web touches the rather limited subset of human experience spent sitting alone staring at a screen. The way we browse the Web, clicking with a mouse, is like what a child does sitting in a shopping cart at a supermarket, pointing at things of interest, perpetually straining to reach treats that are just out of reach. Children at play present a much more compelling metaphor for interacting with information, using all of their senses to explore and create, in groups as well as alone. Anyone who was ever a child understands these skills, but computers don't.

The march of technical progress threatens to turn the simple pleasure of reading a nicely bound book, or writing with a fountain pen, into an antitechnical act of defiance. To keep up, your book should be on a CD-ROM, and your writing should be done with a stylus on a computer's input tablet. But the reality is that books or fountain pens really do perform their intended jobs better than their digital descendants.

Expect More from Computers

This doesn't mean we should throw out our computers; it means we should expect much more from them. As radical as it may sound, it actually is increasingly possible to ask that new technology work as well as what it presumes to replace. We've only recently been able to explain why the printing on a sheet of paper looks so much better than the same text on a computer screen, and are just beginning to glimpse how we can use electronic inks to turn paper itself into a display so that the contents of a book can change.

Unless this challenge is taken seriously, the connected digital world will remain full of barriers. A computer with a keyboard and mouse can be used by only one person at a time, helping you communicate with someone on the other side of the world but not with someone in the same room. Inexpensive computers still cost as much as a used car, and are much more difficult to understand how to operate, dividing society into an information-rich upper class and an information-poor underclass. A compact disc player faithfully reproduces the artistic creations of a very small group of people and turns everyone else into passive consumers. We live in a three-dimensional world, but displays and printers restrict information to two-dimensional surfaces. A desktop computer requires a desk, and a laptop computer requires a lap, forcing you to sit still. Either you can take a walk, or you can use a computer.

These problems can all be fixed by dismantling the real barrier, the one between digital information and our physical world. We're made out of atoms, and will continue to be for the foreseeable future. All of the bits in the world are of no use unless they can meet us out here on our terms. The very notion that computers can create a virtual reality requires an awkward linguistic construction to refer to "real" reality, what's left outside the computer. That's backward. Rather than replace our world, we should first look to machines to enhance it.

The Digital Revolution is an incomplete story. There is a disconnect between the breathless pronouncements of cyber gurus and the experience of ordinary people left perpetually upgrading hardware to meet the demands of new software, or wondering where their files have gone, or trying to understand why they can't connect to the network. The revolution so far has been for the computers, not the people.

Digital Data

Digital data of all kinds, whether an e-mail message or a movie, is encoded as a string of 0's and 1's because of a remarkable discovery by Claude Shannon and John von Neumann in the 1940s. Prior to their work, it was obvious that engineered systems degraded with time and use. A tape recording sounds worse after it is duplicated, a photocopy is less satisfactory than an original, a telephone call becomes more garbled the farther it has to travel. They showed that this is not so for a digital representation. Errors still occur in digital systems, but instead of continuously degrading the performance there is a threshold below which errors can be corrected with near certainty. This means that you can send a message to the next room, or to the next planet, and be confident that it will arrive in the form in which you sent it. In fact, our understanding of how to correct errors has improved so quickly over time that it has enabled deep-space probes to continue sending data at the same rate even though their signals have been growing steadily weaker.

The same digital error correction argument applies to manipulating and storing information. A computer can be made out of imperfect components yet faithfully execute a sequence of instructions for as long as is needed. Data can be saved to a medium that is sure to degrade, but be kept in perpetuity as long as it is periodically copied with error correction. Although no one knows how long a single CD will last, our society can leave a permanent legacy that will outlast any stone tablet as long as someone or something is around to do a bit of regular housekeeping.

In the 1980s at centers such as MIT's Media Lab, people realized that the implications of a digital representation go far beyond reliability: content can transcend its physical representation. At the time ruinous battles were being fought over formats for electronic media such as videotapes (Sony's Betamax vs. Matsushita's VHS) and high-definition television (the United States vs. Europe vs. Japan). These were analog formats, embodied in the custom circuitry needed to decode them. Because hardware sales were tied to the format, control over the standards was seen as the path to economic salvation.

Decoding Data

These heated arguments missed the simple observation that a stream of digital data could equally well represent a video, or some text, or a computer program. Rather than decide in advance which format to use, data can be sent with the instructions for a computer to decode them so that anyone is free to define a new standard without needing new hardware. The consumers who were supposed to be buying high-definition television sets from the national champions are instead buying PCs to access the Web.

The protocols of the Internet now serve to eliminate rather than enforce divisions among types of media. Computers can be connected without regard to who made them or where they are, and information can be connected without needing to artificially separate sights and sounds, content and context. The one minor remaining incompatibility is with people.

Those Dumb Boxes

Billions of dollars are spent developing powerful processors that are put into dumb boxes that have changed little from the earliest days of computing. Yet for so many people and so many applications, the limitation is the box, not the processor. Most computers are nearly blind, deaf, and dumb. These inert machines channel the richness of human communication through a keyboard and a mouse. The speed of the computer is increasingly much less of a concern than the difficulty in telling it what you want it to do, or in understanding what it has done, or in using it where you want to go rather than where it can go.

More transistors are being put on a chip, more lines of code are being added to programs, more computers are appearing on the desks in an office, but computers are not getting easier to use and workers are not becoming more productive. An army of engineers is continuing to solve these legacy problems from the early days of computing, when what's needed is better integration between computers and the rest of the world.

The essential division in the industry between hardware and software represents the organization of computing from the system designer's point of view, not the user's. In successful mature technologies it's not possible to isolate the form and the function. The logical design and the mechanical design of a pen or a piano bind their mechanism with their user interface so closely that it's possible to use them without thinking of them as technology, or even thinking of them at all.

Invisible Computing

Invisibility is the missing goal in computing. Information technology is at an awkward developmental stage where it is adept at communicating its needs and those of other people, but not yet able to anticipate yours. From here we can either unplug everything and go back to an agrarian society—an intriguing but unrealistic option—or we can bring so much technology so close to people that it can finally disappear. Beyond seeking to make computers ubiquitous, we should try to make them unobtrusive.

A VCR insistently flashing 12:00 is annoying, but notice that it doesn't know that it is a VCR, that the job of a VCR is to tell the time rather than ask it, that there are atomic clocks available on the Internet that can give it the exact time, or even that you might have left the room and have no interest in what it thinks the time is. As we increasingly cohabit with machines, we are doomed to be frustrated by our creations if they lack the rudimentary abilities we take for granted—having an identity, knowing something about our environment, and being able to communicate. In return, these machines need to be designed with the presumption that it is their job to do what we want, not the converse. Like my computer, my children started life by insisting that I provide their inputs and collect their outputs, but unlike my computer they are now learning how to do these things for themselves.

What People Do Best

Fixing the division of labor between people and machines depends on understanding what each does best. One day I came into my lab and found all my students clustered around a PC. From the looks on their faces I could tell that this was one of those times when the world had changed. This was when it had just become possible to add a camera and microphone to a computer and see similarly equipped people elsewhere. There was a reverential awe as live faces would pop up on the screen. An early Internet cartoon showed two dogs typing at a computer, one commenting to the other that the great thing about the Internet was that no one could tell that they were dogs. Now we could.

And the dogs were right. The next day the system was turned off, and it hasn't been used since. The ghostly faces on the screen couldn't compete with the resolution, refresh rate, three-dimensionality, color fidelity, and relevance of the people outside of the screen. My students found that the people around them were generally much more interesting than the ones on the screen.

It's no accident that one of the first Web celebrities was a thing, not a person. A camera trained on the coffeepot in the Computer Science department at Cambridge University was connected to a Web server that could show you the state of the coffeepot, timely information of great value (if you happen to be in the department and want a cup of coffee).

A Cup of Coffee

Even better would be for the coffee machine to check when you want coffee, rather than the other way around. If your coffee cup could measure the temperature and volume of your coffee, and relay that information to a computer that kept track of how much coffee you drank at what times, it could do a pretty good job of guessing when you would be coming by for a refill. This does not require sticking a PC into the cup; it is possible to embed simple materials in it that can be sensed from a distance. The data handling is also simple; a lifetime record of coffee drinking is dwarfed by the amount of data in a few moments of video. And it does not require a breakthrough in artificial intelligence to predict coffee consumption.

A grad student in the Media Lab, Joseph Kaye, instrumented our coffee machine and found the unsurprising result that there's a big peak in consumption in the morning after people get in, and another one in the afternoon after lunch. He went further to add electronic tags so that the coffee machine could recognize individual coffee cups and thereby give you the kind of coffee you prefer, along with relevant news retrieved from a server while you wait. No one of these steps is revolutionary; but taken together their implications are. You get what you want—a fresh cup of coffee—without having to attend to the details. The machines are communicating with each other so that you don't have to.

Computers Should Free People

For all of the coverage of the growth of the Internet and the World Wide Web, a far bigger change is coming as the number of things using the Net dwarfs the number of people. The real promise of connecting computers is to free people, by embedding the means to solve problems in the things around us.

There's some precedent for this kind of organization. The recurring lesson we've learned from the study of biology is that hard problems are solved by the interaction of many simple systems. Biology is very much a bottom-up design that gets updated without a lot of central planning. This does not mean that progress is steady. Far from it; just ask a dinosaur (or a mainframe). Here we come to the real problem with the Digital Revolution. Revolutions break things. Sometimes that's a necessary thing to do, but continuously discarding the old and heralding the new is not a sustainable way to live.

A Digital Evolution

Very few mature technologies become obsolete. Contrary to predictions, radio did not kill off newspapers, because it's not possible to skim through a radio program and flip back and forth to parts of interest. Television similarly has not eliminated radio, because there are plenty of times when our ears are more available than our eyes. CD-ROMs have made little dent in book publishing because of the many virtues of a printed book. Far more interesting than declaring a revolution is to ask how to capture the essence of what works well in the present in order to improve the future.

The real challenge is to figure out how to create systems with many components that can work together and change. We've had a digital revolution; we now need digital evolution. . . . The machines have had their turn; now it's ours.

Tomorrow's "Smart" Technologies Will Improve Everyday Life

Susan L. Crowley

After consulting almost two dozen expert sources, Susan L. Crowley, a senior editor on the staff of the *AARP Bulletin*, wrote this 2000 forecast of how "smart" technologies will change and enhance people's lives in the future. She elicited some very rosy predictions. Brainy robots and smart houses will improve life at home and at work. How people travel, how they fight diseases and aging, and how they entertain themselves will all be transformed by computers and the Internet. Some of these developments may not be realized for about fifty years, but others are expected to happen in less than a decade.

CONSIDER THE POSSIBILITIES: ROBOTS TO CLEAN your house and your arteries. Signet rings that hold your bank records. Surgery performed in your living room. Luxury hotels in space.

Pretty dazzling ideas, and many of them not so far off. After all, driven by curiosity and an awe of the unknown, we have long sought to understand and control our environment, our health, our very existence.

The result has been a steady flow throughout history of increasingly sophisticated technologies. And the odds are, say

■

From "Hello to Our Future," by Susan L. Crowley, *AARP Bulletin*, January 2000. Reprinted by permission of the *AARP Bulletin*.

experts and forecasters the *AARP Bulletin* consulted for this article, people in the new century won't be disappointed with the upcoming array of show-stopping gizmos and "smart" technologies intended to improve everyday life.

Even so, "it is difficult to predict how these things will change people's lives," says Michael Coen of the Massachusetts Institute of Technology. "Who could have predicted indoor plumbing, which changed the world?"

It helps to remember, too, that advances in technology and science do not march along in a continuum. There will surely be bumps on the road to a more perfect world.

Figuring out how to foot the bill may slow things down. So will breakthroughs that turn out to be false starts, sending researchers back to the lab.

Then there are the unforeseen disasters—earthquakes, floods, perhaps a virus toxic enough to harm millions of people. Or catastrophic war.

Human Nature May Be Biggest Obstacle

The biggest—and most unpredictable—bump of all may be the contrariness of human nature. While we yearn for the convenience and helpfulness of high-tech marvels, many of us may be unwilling to give up our books for words on a screen or a live Broadway show for the virtual-reality version.

We are apt to balk at the electronic invasion of privacy. Videophones failed to catch on because they're intrusive—people don't want to be seen on the phone in their underwear. How, then, will we feel about smart walls that chart our every move, even if for our own safety and comfort?

Technology may extend human life spans by years, even decades. "But do you really want to remain married to your spouse for 90 years?" asks William B. Schwartz, M.D., of the University of Southern California.

We may wish to stop pain or aging, but will we be put off by the thought of tiny devices roaming through our bodies making tissue repairs? Artificial-intelligence expert Ray Kurzweil predicts computers will be able to calculate as well as the human brain by 2019, but do we want machines smarter than we are?

Finally, we will have to wrestle with moral and ethical questions. Will new technologies further divide rich from poor? Will they be used for malevolent purposes?

As commentator Meg Greenfield pointed out in 1997, in the new millennium "science/technology will be different. Its human manipulators, subjects and beneficiaries won't."

Yet whether you greet the new age with grins or grumbles, it's important to look ahead. Science and technology "decide the kind of futures that are possible," writes distinguished science fiction author Arthur C. Clarke. "Human wisdom must decide which are desirable."

Some new technologies could be available within a few years, some not for decades. How will they change the daily life of you and yours? Scientists don't necessarily agree on what the future holds, but here are some best guesses, based on current research:

Smart Homes

Yes, we may at last have robots picking up after us. But eventually housekeeping will go beyond robotics and computers toward "invisibility."

The power of artificial intelligence will be pervasive but unseen—built into materials or piped into homes, as electricity is now. The goal is labor-saving devices that need no programming, no switches, no batteries.

Clarke has predicted that homes will even evolve to the point where they are "completely self-contained and mobile, so they can be moved to any spot on Earth within 24 hours."

Other Forecasts:

- The "intelligent room" will have walls that can "see" you by sensors, "hear" you by voice recognition systems and "speak" to you in response to your requests.
- Most household equipment, from lights to toasters, will respond to voice commands. In an emergency, you'll call into the air, "Get the ambulance!" and it will be done.
- Today's techno-clutter will vanish. An all-purpose screen, flat to the wall, will "converse" with you on the stock market; diagnose failures of in-house systems; conjure up relatives in Australia so they can join you for dinner in "real time."
- Smart cupboards and fridges will automatically reorder

foods that run out. Clothing and household linens will be made of smart fabrics that clean and press themselves, making washing machines and ironing boards oddities of the past.

- Bathroom surfaces will repel mold and scum. Tubs and showers will give way to "human washing machines": plastic pods (already used in Japan) that cycle you through a soaping, washing, rinsing and drying—sauna or Jacuzzi style.
- Electronic wallpaper will let you change the color or pattern of your walls instantly. Electronic image spots will display Van Goghs or any other art you dial up.
- Keys, locks and bolts will become antiques. You will enter and exit by voice command. "Open Sesame" will become reality.

The Workplace

As we leave the Industrial Revolution further behind and move deeper into the era of technological wizardry, the workplace will undergo seismic changes.

The new millennium, says Jeremy Rifkin, founder of the Foundation on Economic Trends in Washington, will "signal the beginning of a new era in history in which human beings are liberated, at long last, from a life of backbreaking toil and mindless repetitive tasks." What might happen to the work world?

- Automation and online transactions will eliminate middlemen—telephone operators, bank tellers, travel booking agents, among others—and middle managers.
- More teachers, therapists, caregivers, golf pros and other personal-service workers will be needed for jobs requiring the judgment that robots don't have. Repair people will be needed to fix the robots when, inevitably, they break down.
- Increasingly, robots will "man" factory assembly lines. They will tailor products—everything from the design of your car to the fit of your clothes—to your personal specifications. Materials, from steel to denim, will be built atom by atom, under the control of nanocomputers [extremely small].
- You won't get your hands as dirty as today's workers, but your working years will extend well beyond theirs. You will

constantly learn new skills and have a variety of careers.
- You will seldom commute, since your office will be wherever you are—at home, in the Alps, at the bowling alley. You will stay in touch via "hologram" sessions, where projected images of people in different locations come together. You need not be there in the flesh—your programmed image will speak for you.

Once liberated from a life of toil, what then? Join "the search for knowledge and the creation of beauty," suggests Clarke.

Getting Around

Our favorite way of getting around, by car, hasn't changed much in the last century and won't in this one. Cars of the future will be made of molded plastic and powered by nonpolluting fuels. Other changes:
- Motor vehicles will run on magnetized tracks on the interstates, traveling bumper to bumper at 100–200 m.p.h., with no real driving involved. Dashboard computers will warn of accidents and delays en route and tell the location of the nearest open parking spot. Parking signs, meters and tollbooths will vanish.
- Onboard computers will monitor the workings of your auto and diagnose incipient or actual failures, automatically informing the shop of spare parts you'll need.
- Aircraft will take off vertically, reducing noise and the size of airports.
- Orbiting the Earth will be the first space cruise open to tourists. You'll rise from ground to satellite via a space elevator, soaring up a tethered cable that generates its own energy.

Orbiting hotels will quickly follow. Honeymoons in space will be the ultimate status symbol—till a new fad comes along.

Health and Medicine

Almost everyone agrees that Americans born in the next century will live a lot longer than age 77, today's average life expectancy. While the U.S. Census Bureau conservatively puts the average life span for a person born in 2050 at 85 years, others say that huge leaps in medicine will enable many people to live to 120, or older.

"Regenerative medicine, tissue-based medicine and geriatric medicine will be the three major fields of the 21st century," noted geriatrician Robert Butler, M.D., says.

Some Faulty Forecasts

Some people might be better off staying out of the prediction game, such as the flummoxed forecasters quoted in "The Experts Speak: The Definitive Compendium of Authoritative Misinformation," by Christopher Cerf and Victor Navasky:

Electric light: ". . . good enough for our transatlantic friends . . . but unworthy of the attention of practical or scientific men," British Parliament report on Edison's work, 1878.

The telephone: "That's an amazing invention, but who would ever want to use one of them?" President Rutherford Hayes, 1876.

Television: "People will soon get tired of staring at a plywood box every night," Darryl F. Zanuck, head of Twentieth Century-Fox, circa 1946.

Computers: "There is no reason for any individual to have a computer in their home," Ken Olson, president of Digital Equipment Corporation, 1977.

Aviation: "The popular mind often pictures gigantic flying machines speeding across the Atlantic and carrying innumerable passengers . . . It seems safe to say that such ideas are wholly visionary," Harvard astronomer William Henry Pickering, 1908.

Nuclear energy: "Nuclear powered vacuum cleaners will probably be a reality within 10 years," vacuum cleaner manufacturer Alex Lewyt, 1955.

Medicine: "The abdomen, the chest, and the brain will be forever shut from the intrusion of the wise and humane surgeon," leading British surgeon Sir John Erichsen, 1837.

Susan L. Crowley, *AARP Bulletin*, January 2000.

And yes, even with razzle-dazzle technology expected to come on line over the next 100 years, you will still have to exercise and eat your vegetables (whether in pill form or their natural state) for good health.

Future Health Trends

Here's what may lie ahead, in the next 10 to 100 years:

- A scan of your genetic structure (with billions of bits of data about the estimated 80,000 genes in your body) will detect symptoms or susceptibility to particular diseases.
- Nanobots—miniscule robots— will deliver medications to affected cells to prevent or treat disease. Or they will clear clogged arteries or repair damaged tissue.
- You can have your checkup anywhere, anytime. You can have your vital signs tested by machines at the drugstore and send the results to your doctor via the Internet for analysis.
- Hospitals will fade away. A surgeon in Boston will do your hip replacement at your home in Cleveland via virtual reality. The doctor will view the surgical site on a screen and remotely manipulate surgical instruments inserted by a technician.
- Implanted biochips will monitor your vital signs, alerting you or your doctor to an impending crisis.
- Replacing diseased or worn-out body parts will be as routine as replacing auto parts today.
- Most diseases will be cured, perhaps with one exception. "I think we'll cure cancer before we cure the common cold," says Francis Collins, M.D., director of the National Human Genome Research Institute.

Entertainment and Leisure

"Leisure-oriented businesses," futurist Graham T.T. Molitor wrote in *The Futurist*, "will account for 50 percent of the U.S. gross national product shortly after 2015."

And with people then devoting more than half their time to leisure, what they will want is to be entertained—lavishly. They should be pleased with the whiz-bang amusements that virtual reality and artificial intelligence will bring:

- In the near future: one remote, one screen and no channels at all. Forget real time. On Monday at 3 a.m., you can call up the Broadway opening of "A Chorus Line" (or scan a list of offerings). Or watch the 1976 NBA finals, the news, the text of "King Lear" or the first Beatles performance on the Ed Sullivan show.

- Seated in a special chair that senses if you're cold or uncomfortable and adapts accordingly, you pull the bubble-screen down around you. Your computer/ entertainment center can teach you any language you want, produce a jazz bass line to go with your computerized melody or let you play a round of virtual-reality golf.

- Thinking will make it so, says forecaster Kurzweil. The nerve cells of a human brain can be linked to computer circuitry, creating a network that can interact with similar networks, and with computers and other databases. The upshot: Just *think*, for example, of the 1973 World Series or Barbra Streisand singing "The Way We Were," and there it will be. One possible kink yet to be resolved: The contents of the brain could be scanned and downloaded into an external database, where they could be manipulated, stolen or even erased.

- Expanded leisure will prompt people to continue their educations and solve social problems. Some experts foresee not just technological revolution but a new desire by humans to look inward and to each other for old-fashioned values like peace and contentment.

At the end of the 1990s, while the world buzzed about the coming of the robotized human brain, a book by the Dalai Lama quietly made the bestseller lists.

It's called "The Art of Happiness."

GLOSSARY

analog Information that is presented in a continuous fashion. The hands of a clock, for example, can move in an analog fashion, presenting time in a continuous sweep and showing the time that passes between the distinct minute markers. In contrast, a digital clock presents time as distinct and separate numbers without showing the fractions of minutes that also are passing. The opposite of *analog* is **digital**.

artificial intelligence Also known simply as AI, artificial intelligence models human learning patterns and recognition in computers.

bandwidth The amount of information that can be exchanged between computers in a certain amount of time via a network. A network that can carry large amounts of data quickly is said to have wide bandwidth.

broadband This high-speed, two-way technology delivers high-speed Internet access, local telephone services, and television programming along a single wire that can carry several channels at once. Cable television companies, which had large capacity, two-way lines already installed, were the first to market this service and to offer Internet customers increased speed and efficiency.

browser A software program used to read electronic documents. Netscape Navigator and Internet Explorer are examples of **Web** browsers.

chip Wafer thin and usually made of the material silicon, chips—also known as semiconductors—hold the circuits that work together to perform a set of tasks. Chips, for example, are programmed to run microwaves, fuel injection systems, and a computer's operating system.

CPU The brains of any computer, the central processing unit determines the computing power.

cyberspace Rather than a real place or three-dimensional space, cyberspace is a nebulous "place" where humans and computers interact via networks. The **World Wide Web** and the **Internet** are considered to be cyberspace.

digital The representation of information as discontinuous data that is encoded as strings of 0's and 1's. Computers are digital machines because they only process data as combinations of zeros and ones. The opposite of *digital* is **analog**.

download   To receive a file or program from another computer.

e-mail   Short for "electronic mail," e-mail involves the digital transmission of a message from one person to another using a communication network.

hardware   The physical parts of a computer system, such as the terminal, screen, and circuit board.

hypertext   A database system that enables files of text, graphics, video, and music to be linked together. Because it allows a user to select words or pictures within the document and to link to related information, it provides the basis for the **World Wide Web.**

Internet   A worldwide system of thousands of interconnected networks that share a common computer language. This branching complex of networks makes it possible for millions of computers to be connected and to transmit data to each other.

intranet   A private network accessed only by selected users.

microprocessor   A silicon **chip** that contains a **CPU.** In the world of personal computers, the terms microprocessor and CPU are interchangeable.

Net   In general, this widely used term refers to the worldwide network of millions of computers that are linked—or networked—to each other. Some people also refer to this network as the Information Highway or as **cyberspace.** The term is not interchangeable with **Internet.** Like the term **cyberspace,** *Net* is meant to capture the imagination and to suggest another world or reality where information travels through space.

node   A processing location for the transmission of data that can be a computer or other device. Each node has its own address on the network; and on large networks, data is moved along from node to node until it reaches its destination.

packet   On the **Internet,** messages are divided into more than one packet before being sent along the network to their destination. Each of the packets contains the destination address and can travel over different networks—depending on the network traffic and operations. Once they reach their destination, the packets are reassembled into the original message and delivered, for example, to an **e-mail** account.

platform   A computer's operating system, which can include both its **hardware** and **software**.

protocol   A definition, a standard, or an agreed-upon set of rules designed to let different computers and different networks communicate with each other worldwide.

server The device or computer system that enables other computers or devices to link to the network and to communicate with each other. A computer-based communications system can have several servers, such as a file server, mail server, or network server to help in accessing files, e-mail, or other networks.

software A computer program that enables the computer to perform a certain function. Unlike a computer's hardware, the software is not physically tangible.

URL The Uniform Resource Locator is the address for items locatable via the **World Wide Web.**

virtual reality Like **cyberspace** or the **Net**, this term refers to a place that does not exist in actual fact or form. Instead, people enter or "live in" a virtual place after hooking up to a computer that creates sensory illusions that the user experiences as "real."

World Wide Web Also known as the WWW, the W3, or the Web, this collection of millions of computer sites can be accessed by any computer that has a Web **browser** and access to the **Internet**. Instead of coming from one central location, the Web is an assortment of worldwide links that enable people and organizations to communicate with one another and to share data files that can include text, sound, graphics, and other pieces of information.

FOR FURTHER RESEARCH

Books

John Alderman, *Sonic Boom: Napster, MP3 and the New Pioneers of Music.* New York: Perseus Press, 2001.
This was one of the first books to cover the controversy surrounding downloadable music.

David Bell and Barbara M. Kennedy, eds., *The Cybercultures Reader.* New York: Routledge, 2000.
Essays in this anthology discuss topics such as feminism, sexuality, posthumanism, and human-machine interaction in the context of new technologies.

Tim Berners-Lee, *Weaving the Web: The Original Design and Ultimate Destiny of the World Wide Web by Its Inventor.* New York: HarperCollins, 1999.
Tim Berners-Lee believes the Web belongs to the people of the world, not to a single company. The book gives readers insights not only into the process of creating the Web, but also into the inventor's philosophy about what it is and must continue to be.

Frances Cairncross, *The Death of Distance: How the Communications Revolution Will Change Our Lives.* Boston: Harvard Business School Press, 2001.
Cairncross argues that the growing ease and speed of communications will make geographical boundaries obsolete, fundamentally altering the way people think of home, work, and government.

Ann Cavoukian and Don Tapscott, *Who Knows: Safeguarding Your Privacy in a Networked World.* New York: McGraw-Hill, 1997.
Though a bit dated, this book offers good background information for understanding how networked systems operate and how they pass along information.

Michael L. Dertouzos, *The Unfinished Revolution: Human-Centered Computers and What They Can Do for Us.* New York: HarperCollins, 2001.
The author details how more user-friendly computers could im-

prove health care, commerce, disaster control, medicine in developing countries, financial services, and play.

Mark Dery, *Escape Velocity: Cyberculture at the End of the Century.* New York: Grove Press, 1996.
Dery explores the world of cyberpunks, cyberhippies, and cyber-sexers—people who are eager for the day when computer technology is merged with the human body.

Katie Hafner and Matthew Lyon, *Where Wizards Stay Up Late.* New York: Simon & Schuster, 1999.
This is the human side of the story about the precursor to today's e-mail system and about the Internet's first virtual community.

Andrew Herman and Thomas Swiss, eds., *The World Wide Web and Contemporary Cultural Theory: Magic, Metaphor, Power.* New York: Routledge, 2000.
The essays in this anthology explore how economic, political, social, and aesthetic forces are shaping the culture of the World Wide Web.

Raymond Kurzweil, *The Age of Intelligent Machines.* Cambridge, MA: MIT Press, 1990.
This is the first of Kurzweil's two books that explore computers—their history and their impact. Both are visually interesting and include a variety of contributing writers.

——, *The Age of Spiritual Machines: When Computers Exceed Human Intelligence.* New York: Viking, 1999.
The second of his books focuses less on the history of computers and more on the impact they have on the human mind and spirit. It includes an excellent glossary and a detailed timeline of machines and their arrivals.

Janet H. Murray, *Hamlet on the Holodeck: The Future of Narrative in Cyberspace.* Cambridge, MA: MIT Press, 1998.
The author explores the ways in which computer technology may change storytelling, covering topics such as interactive stories, stories-as-games, and the downsides of interactive escapism.

Steven Poole, *Trigger Happy: Videogames and the Entertainment Revolution.* New York: Arcade, 2000.
The author provides a detailed history of the video game industry along with a discussion of the growing appeal of interactive entertainment.

Mark Poster, *What's the Matter with the Internet?* Minneapolis, MN: University of Minnesota Press, 2001.

The author shares his views on how the Internet will redefine culture and politics and why it is capable of transforming the way people see the world and themselves.

Gregory J.E. Rawlins, *Moths to the Flame: The Seductions of Computer Technology.* Cambridge, MA: MIT Press, 1996.

The publisher offers the interesting option of reading the entire book online at http://archives.obs-us.com/obs/english/books/rawlins/moths.

Douglas S. Robertson, *The New Renaissance: Computers and the Next Level of Civilization.* New York: Oxford University Press, 1998.

Robertson argues that computers will create an information explosion and alter human history as the invention of language, writing, and printing did in previous eras.

David Shenk, *The End of Patience: Cautionary Notes on the Information Revolution.* Bloomington: Indiana University Press, 1999.

Shenk warns that society is headed toward "information overload," the overwhelming sense that modern media technologies churn out more words and images than our culture can usefully absorb.

Don Tapscott, *Growing Up Digital: The Rise of the Net Generation.* New York: McGraw Hill, 1998.

Tapscott coined the term "Net Generation," and contends the people in this generation far surpass all others in their technical savvy.

Brian Winston, *Media Technology and Society: A History: From the Telegraph to the Internet.* New York: Routledge, 1998.

Winston traces the development of communications technologies—from the telegraph and the telephone to computers, satellites, and virtual reality—with emphasis on how each has benefited and disrupted society.

William Wresch, *Disconnected: Haves and Have-Nots in the Information Age.* New Brunswick, NJ: Rutgers University Press, 1996.

Wresch explores a major problem of the Information Revolution—the fact that, due to deeply entrenched socioeconomic problems, most people are missing out on its benefits.

Periodicals

Robert Buderi, "The Virus Wars," *Atlantic Monthly*, April 1999.

Christopher Conte, "How Access Benefits Children: Connecting Our Kids to the World of Information," National Telecommunications and Information Administration of the U.S. Department of Commerce, September 1999. Available at www.ntia.doc.gov/otiahome/top/publicationmedia/How_ABC/ How_ABC.html.

Philip Elmer-Dewitt, "On a Screen Near You: Cyberporn," *Time*, July 3, 1995.

Alex Gove, "Fight the Power: Chuck D Speaks Out on the Artist's Role in E-Commerce," *Red Herring Magazine*, December 1999.

Karl Taro Greenfeld, "Meet the Napster," *Time*, October 2, 2000. Go to www.time.com/time/magazine/articles/0,3266,55730-1,00. html for this article and links to other Napster-related topics.

Amy Harmon, "Researchers Find Sad, Lonely World in Cyberspace," *New York Times*, August 30, 1998.

Doug Isenberg, "MP3 and Napster: The Day the Copyright Died?" *Internet World*, September 1, 2000.

Jake Kirchner, "The Web's Hip-Hop Future," *PC Magazine*, August 1, 1999.

Toby Lester, "The Reinvention of Privacy," *Atlantic Monthly*, March 2001.

Charles Mann, "The Heavenly Jukebox," *Atlantic Monthly*, September 2000.

Jakob Nielsen, "Loneliness and the Internet," *ZDNet Developer*, February 20, 2000. This article, plus other links to the Stanford University Study on the Internet and Isolation, can be found at http://web.zdnet.com/devhead/alertbox.

Rod Norland and Jeffrey Bartholet, "The Web's Dirty Secret," a *Newsweek* special report on pedophiles on the Internet, March 13, 2001.

Robert J. Samuelson, "The Internet and Gutenberg," *Newsweek*, January 24, 2000.

Bruce Sterling, "Will Cyber Criminals Run the World?" *Time*, June 19, 2000.

David Streitfeld, "A Web of Workaholic Misfits? Study Finds Internet Users Are Socially Isolated," *Washington Post*, February 16, 2000.

Stuart Taylor Jr., "Is It Sexual Exploitation if Victims Are 'Virtual'?" *Newsweek*, March 19, 2001.

Timothy L. Thomas, "Preventing Conflict Through Information Technology," *Military Review*, December–February 1999. Available at www.cgsc.army.mil/milrev/English/DecFeb99/thomas.htm.

William Bennett Turner, "What Part of 'No Law' Don't You Understand?" *Wired*, March 1996.

Anthony Walton, "Technology Versus African Americans," *Atlantic Monthly*, January 1999.

Web Resources

American Civil Liberties Union
www.aclu.org/issues/cyber/hmcl.html
The American Civil Liberties Union believes that cyberspace must be kept free from censorship and government controls. This website provides up-to-date links to discussions on censorship, privacy, and related court cases.

Carnegie Mellon University
http://homenet.andrew.cmu.edu/progress/
Since 1995, the university's HomeNet Project has studied the use of the Internet at home. The researchers documented how family members use online services such as electronic mail, computerized bulletin boards, online chat groups, and the World Wide Web. The HomeNet web site links to current articles and research on the topic.

The Internet Society (ISOC)
www.isoc.org/isoc/
www.isoc.org/internet/history/
The Internet Society is made up of more than 150 organizational and 6,000 individual members in over 100 countries. The ISOC website's history link offers an impressive assortment of information on the Internet and the Web.

The Living Internet
http://livinginternet.com/
Launched in January 2000, this site describes itself as the most comprehensive reference about the Internet. It also offers information about the World Wide Web, e-mail, and newsgroups and is updated weekly.

National Telecommunications and Information Administration (NTIA)
www.ntia.doc.gov
The National Telecommunications and Information Administration, a division of the U.S. Department of Commerce, is an excellent resource for information about computers, the Internet, the World Wide Web and their use and impact. For example, the full report *Falling Through the Net: Defining the Digital Divide*, a portion of which appears in this book, can be downloaded from this site.

World Wide Web Consortium
www.w3.org
www.w3.org/People/Berners-Lee/Overview.html
This website provides ongoing and updated information about the World Wide Web Consortium. Here you will also find information about Tim Berners-Lee, the Web's inventor and advocate. By going directly to the Berners-Lee pages within the W3, you will find a variety of links that will take you to talks Berners-Lee has given, details about his projects, and his views of the consortium and its work.

INDEX